From Homemaker to Breadwinner

How to Make It BIG in Real Estate Sales

Myra Nourmand

From Homemaker to Breadwinner:
How to Make It BIG in Real Estate Sales

Copyright © 2008 by Myra Nourmand

First edition 2008
Printed and bound in the United States of America

Library of Congress Control Number 2007904425
ISBN: 978-0-9797730-0-6 Hardcover
ISBN: 978-0-9797730-1-3 Paperback

Production coordinated by Lawrence Ineno
Cover design by Howard Nourmand

Published by Nourmand & Associates Inc.
421 North Beverly Drive, Suite 200, Beverly Hills, CA 90210.

Acknowledgements

For my parents Yetta and Arnold, whom I watched and from whom I learned, and who instilled the belief in me that in America, anything is possible.

To my husband, Saeed, my teacher and mentor. Thank you for your unflagging support, which I can sum up with your words: "You sold me, Myra—you can sell the world."

My three shining diamonds—Nicole, Howard, and Michael—who have given me more happiness than stars in the sky.

To my countless family members whose trials and tribulations have taught me to maneuver through life's complex family situations.

Thank you Victoria Peters and Wilma Winer, whose organizational skills and incredible dedication keep me running in the right direction.

And special thanks to Lawrence Ineno. Your collaboration and expertise have been invaluable to this project.

*This book is dedicated to the late Robert K. Nourmand,
my father-in-law, whose charm, laughter, sense of family, and
strong work ethic have been my inspiration.*

Table of Contents

INTRODUCTION

FROM BUFFALO TO BEVERLY HILLS   11

CHAPTER 1

WHAT BRINGS YOU HERE?   27

CHAPTER 2

ARE YOU READY TO BE A SALES SUPERSTAR?   39

CHAPTER 3

EXPERT STATUS IS THE FAST TRACK TO SUCCESS   49

CHAPTER 4

HOW TO FIND A BUYER'S DREAM HOME, EVEN WHEN IT WASN'T
WHAT SHE WAS DREAMING ABOUT   63

CHAPTER 5

THE ART OF TELLING YOUR CLIENTS THAT THEIR PERFECT
HOME AIN'T SO PERFECT   73

CHAPTER 6
HOW TO STAGE A HOME TO SELL: APPEALING TO ALL THE SENSES   81

CHAPTER 7
THE FOUR D'S OF REAL ESTATE: DIVORCE, DEBT, DEATH & DESIRE   91

CHAPTER 8
"WHAT DO YOU MEAN, THE PATIO FURNITURE ISN'T INCLUDED?"
KEYS TO SUCCESSFUL NEGOTIATION   105

CHAPTER 9
ADJUSTING TO CHANGE: COMBINING TODAY'S TECHNOLOGY
WITH OLD-FASHIONED COMMON SENSE   123

CHAPTER 10
YOU CAN'T CLAP WITH ONE HAND: SUCCESS TAKES TEAMWORK   129

INDEX   145

Introduction:
From Buffalo to Beverly Hills

Everyone has 24 hours in a day. Not even the President of the United States gets 28 or 30 hours. So delegate and prioritize intelligently.

— *Saeed Nourmand*

My husband is passionate about real estate. An engineer turned entrepreneur, Saeed has lived and breathed it since 1976. Once in a while, he'll spot a house that he thinks I would love to live in. Without even looking at it, I always tell him no. I attribute my aversion to moving to my childhood. From my birth in Germany until Saeed and I settled in Los Angeles, I had moved 11 times. I felt like I had done enough moving for a lifetime, and it also explains why I've lived in the same house for the last 26 years.

Although I was born in Germany, my stay was brief. At the time, my parents were living there partly by choice but mostly out of necessity. After being liberated from the Nazi concentration camps in their native Poland, they relocated to Germany. It was there that my parents, Henry and Yetta, met. Henry was fifteen years older than his bride-to-be. He was tall, handsome, and debonair. As they dated, he promised Yetta that once they were married, he would take her to the United States where he would provide for her, and together they would realize the American Dream.

In 1946, the couple married, and they immediately focused on their mission: Move to the United States. For them, this country was a place where they could leave behind the horrors of Hitler's Final Solution and begin their new lives.

Meanwhile, my mother's aunt was living in New Jersey. Tanta Minnie, as I called her, was taking care of the paperwork that would allow my mother and her family to immigrate to the United States.

When I was 22 months old, Tanta Minnie's hard work prevailed. She became the legal sponsor of the newlyweds, and they gained entry into this country. Yetta and Henry packed their belongings, which were few, considering that the Nazis had pillaged their possessions. Then, with their infant daughter, they set off for the United States. So begins the story of recovery, renewal, and success despite staggering odds.

SIX YEARS IN THE UNITED STATES

My parents were strong people. They had survived one of the most horrific events of the 20th century and lived to talk about it. The experience of being in a concentration camp motivated them to rise above those whose goal was to annihilate them. Once in New Jersey, they immediately found work, which meant that they had to send their baby daughter to day care. At the time, this was something uncommon for Eastern European parents to do.

My father's first job was in a dairy. Meanwhile, my mother worked in a factory sewing dresses. Before her morning commute by bus, she took me to day care. Because she didn't drive, she pushed a stroller through snow, rain, or heat, and dropped me off at the childcare center. From there, she waited for a bus that would take her to the factory. At the end of the day, after hours of intense work, she would repeat the process: bus ride, day care, and then a walk home.

From the beginning, my parents lived frugally because they were intent on purchasing a home. Once they saved enough, they invested in a two-story property. The three of us lived on the first floor while a family rented the room upstairs. Little did I know that my parents' understanding of the benefits of homeownership would guide my career choice many years later.

As a result of his success, my father bought his own dairy business. At home, we had what seemed like an endless supply of eggs, milk, butter, and cheese. By the time I was five, I had already consumed a lifetime's worth of dairy products, which probably explains why I don't care for them today.

The business grew, and he took on a partner to share the responsibilities. My parents were reaching their goals and became respected members of society. In 1954, all three of us became naturalized citizens. My father then secured a driver's license and declared his fulfillment of the American Dream by buying a car—a shiny, new black Buick.

My father had kept the promise he made to his wife several years ago in Germany. They were established in their new country, and he was a successful entrepreneur. Although the war had stripped him of everything he valued, he maintained an insatiable hope for the future and a commitment to his family.

On Thanksgiving Day, 1954, my parents and I were on our way to dinner at the home of my father's business partner.

I recall sitting in the back seat surrounded by other cars—all of us driving to our Thanksgiving Day destinations. Suddenly, our new Buick stopped. In the middle of traffic, my father abruptly grabbed the gearshift and shifted it into Park. Without saying a word, he put his head down.

My mother shook his shoulder back and forth. His head, however, remained planted on the headrest. Traffic signals changed from red to green. Horns blared behind us. Surrounding cars moved ahead and swerved around ours. But my father's unconscious state remained the same. My mother let out a scream—a visceral cry that I'll never forget.

To this day, I don't know how they found out, but eventually I heard the shrill of a siren. I was only six years old, so I did my best to explain to the paramedics what had happened. They carried my father out of the car, and we took a seat in the ambulance.

Once we arrived at the hospital, I sat in the waiting room while my mother remained with my father. Eventually, she emerged from the hospital room and sat next to me. Her eyes were filled with tears, and her hands were full. In her fists, she clutched a watch, a wedding band, and a wallet. My father had suffered a fatal coronary heart attack, and these were the three possessions that he carried with him.

Grieving was a luxury my mother could not afford. The bills had to be paid, and her daughter had to be raised. For the next two years, she worked as a single mother to support both of us.

From that Thanksgiving forward, we stopped celebrating the holiday. Year after year, I remember sitting in class and listening to my teachers talk about Thanksgiving. "It's a time to give thanks," they would say. Meanwhile, it was a day about which we never spoke at home and an event that brought about one of the biggest changes of my life.

It wasn't until I married Saeed that Thanksgiving was restored to its celebratory status. We were looking to live in Beverly Hills at the time, and I was pregnant with our second son, Michael. It was a big move—from our simple residence to our estate in the best part of Beverly Hills. We finally found a home that we loved.

Unfortunately, competition was fierce, and our chances for an accepted offer were slim. The other buyers were more qualified and had better financial resources than we did. But through Saeed's determination and negotiation skills, he convinced the owner to sell the house to us.

Thanksgiving was rapidly approaching, and Saeed explained to the owner the circumstances behind my father's death. My husband requested to buy the house on Thanksgiving Day. He told the seller that he wanted his wife never to be sad on this day again. The deal was sealed on Thanksgiving; escrow closed two months later, and we moved into our beautiful home on the first day of spring.

A SECOND START IN AMERICA

Like my parents and countless other Jews who had survived Nazi Germany, Arnold arrived in the United States with few belongings and a determination to succeed. My mother's sister, Anne, knew Arnold's sister. Both sisters felt that my mother and Arnold shared much in common. Two years after my father's death, Anne acted as a matchmaker and convinced my mother and Arnold to meet. My aunt Anne saw an opportunity to improve my mother's life and acted on her behalf.

My mother and Arnold became good friends. They had much in common: their European roots, their native languages, a commitment to family, and a common experience of wartime tragedy. In 1956, they married. The three of us—Arnold, my mother, and I—traveled together for their honeymoon. We stayed in the Concord, a hotel tucked away in the Catskill Mountains.

Initially, when I told friends about my mother's plan to re-marry, they asked how I felt about Arnold: How could my father's shoes be filled so quickly? What if I didn't get along with him? But I never had these fears. I was happy for my mother, and Arnold and I immediately formed a bond that, to this day, has remained strong. Two years later, my baby sister, Betty, was born. With her birth, we were four.

For many years, Arnold earned his income selling sewing machines. He often worked at conventions, where he would host a booth demonstrating the superiority of his products. Surrounded by onlookers, he would grasp a piece of fabric, slide it under the machine's needle, press down on the foot pedal, and raise his hands in the air. The machine whirred as its needle bobbed up and down.

My new father sewed pockets on aprons, embroidered designs on cloth, and monogrammed initials—all with hands-free ease. I stood by his side, wearing an apron with a heart-shaped pocket that this marvelous machine had created.

At first, I was a reluctant prop. But my trepidation vanished once I heard the warm words of passers-by. They would tell Arnold what a lovely daughter he had. I realize now that he was teaching me, at a young age, the skills required to sell successfully.

Arnold was a savvy salesperson who knew how to build a business. With the sale of one machine, he bought two more.

Eventually he sold enough machines to be able to lease a sewing machine store. That store's success allowed him to buy another one. He then set his eyes on a new retail endeavor. Arnold pulled together his resources and approached Paul Swado, owner of the well-known Swado's Furniture Store.

Swado's was in the heart of Downtown Buffalo's Polish district. Here, Arnold knew that his ethnic roots would work to his advantage—he shared the same language and culture as the shop's customers. Mr. Swado sold his company to Arnold. Now my father was the owner of one of the busiest furniture shops in Buffalo, New York.

MARRIAGE AND MY MOVE WEST

In 1970, I graduated from State University New York (SUNY-Buffalo) and married Saeed. Shortly after, we planned to move west. Although he could have found work locally, this was never his intention. While we dated, he would tell me, "Myra, read my lips: We're getting married in Buffalo, but after our honeymoon, we're moving to California."

Saeed is a man of his word. After getting married, we packed our lives in our car and drove across the country. At the time, I was selling waterless cookware. It was a job that I began when I was in college. When I told my boss about my plans to leave Buffalo, he was sad to see one of his most productive sales people leave. In fact, he asked me to launch the same cookware business on the west coast.

At first, this sounded like a good idea. I had never been to California and assumed that the cookware business would be an easy endeavor to launch. But once on the west coast, I quickly learned about Southern California commuter life and how the expansive urban landscape made selling waterless cookware a daunting task.

Our drive to California could have been like an extended honeymoon. After all, the cities that line the cross-country trip have filled pages of countless coffee table books and travel guides. Unfortunately, these publications are the only references we have. As a result of our determination to get to the other side of the country, Saeed and I took to the highway, drove 14 hours a day, and stopped only to eat and rest.

When I look back, I see missed opportunities. Now, I have children, grandchildren, a husband, family, work, and friends, which means my life is filled with activity. Then, we were young with few commitments. We could have ambled across the country, stopped to see the sights, and experienced local culture. Instead, with autopilot-like focus, we charged ahead toward our destination.

First we arrived in San Diego. The Californian climate was what we had been yearning for, and we found it. Soon, however, we realized that San Diego was appealing, but if we really wanted to find high-paying work, we had to move to Los Angeles.

We moved north to Woodland Hills, California, and immediately pored over the local newspaper in search of employment and a place to live. At first, we had trouble finding an apartment. The problem wasn't supply—there was plenty of housing. But with no furniture, no jobs, no personal references, and New York license plates, we had difficulty convincing landlords that we would be stable tenants.

We finally found a place to live, and Saeed landed a job with a local engineering firm. At the same time, he was also making arrangements for his family to move to the United States from Iran. Political instability was making life there more and more difficult, and his family knew that trouble was ahead.

Meanwhile, I looked for work in nearby Van Nuys. I gave up cookware sales and entered an employment agency. Scanning the workspace, with its padded cubicles and fluorescent lighting, I saw that I was clearly the youngest person there. At 22 and fresh out of college, I was surrounded by women in their 40s. After interviewing me, the manager asked if I would be interested in becoming a career counselor. "Who would counsel whom?" I thought. After all, I entered the office in search of career guidance myself.

My next significant job came as a result of a car accident that Saeed and I had during a trip to San Diego. After the collision, friends suggested that we meet with an attorney. During our appointment, the lawyer wanted to know details about the accident and what our current employment status was. I let him know that I had recently quit my job because the office had moved too far from my home. He then gave us a chance to ask him questions. Afterwards, the attorney shared that he was impressed with what I had asked regarding the accident.

"Your questions were better than what most attorneys would want to know. Are you sure you're only 24?" I recall him asking.

At the end of the meeting, he offered me a job. "Earlier you said you weren't working...Well, consider yourself employed now," he said. He explained that he had been in search of a legal secretary.

I shared that I knew shorthand but nothing about the legal field. He showed no concern. "I trust my instincts and have a good feeling about you. Don't worry. I'll teach you everything you need to know," he said.

I started work the following week. At his office, I was responsible for transcribing tapes. Every day, I was the first one there. During the first few days, five tapes waited for me on my desk. I slid them into the machine, listened, typed, and completed all of my work by the end of the day.

Soon, there were six tapes, followed by seven. The workload became intense, but I knew that I had a task to complete, and I didn't leave until it was done.

One day a colleague pulled me aside. "Myra, the girls and I have been talking," I recall her saying. "We can't believe that you're doing seven tapes a day. At this rate there'll be eight waiting for you by the end of the week. Honey, slow down."

From that conversation, I discovered that my co-workers were only completing two or three tapes per day–not six or seven. I realized that when I didn't know any better, I exceeded other's expectations of me.

After I became pregnant with my first child, Nicole, the waterless cookware, employment counseling, and legal work were replaced with diapers, children's books, and sleepless nights of motherhood—being a mom was a full-time job.

My maternal responsibilities grew with the birth of Howard and then Michael. I spent the next many years raising my three children. Once they were school age, they were active in sports, music, acting, and art classes. The responsibility of juggling three schedules while making sure that homework was completed and meals were prepared honed my time-management skills—something that would prove invaluable a few years later.

As my children became more independent, Saeed began encouraging me to re-enter the workforce. The thought piqued my interest, but I was reluctant. So many years spent raising my kids made me doubt my ability to succeed at anything else. But my husband knew I had been a successful salesperson throughout my early adult life. I took his encouragement seriously; Saeed had established a real estate brokerage in Beverly Hills, and he was a formidable judge of character.

In 1988, I took the plunge, passed the exam, and became a licensed broker. Since then, I've moved forward with the same determination that pushed my husband and me to drive from Buffalo to San Diego 14 hours at a time. I'm thankful that my husband motivated me to become a broker. As a result, real estate has become one of my life's passions.

Throughout these pages, you'll read about the experiences that shaped my career and what I've learned during my nearly 20 years in this business. I've had my share of disappointments, but the lessons I've learned from my setbacks have made me wonder whether there's such a thing as a bad experience. Based on that perspective, I can confidently say that my successes far outweigh any difficulties, and my accomplishments have greatly surpassed all my expectations.

Whether you're a mother of three who has never sold a piece of property in your life or a seasoned professional, there's something in here for you. In this book, you'll read about my method to success in real estate sales. This business can be complicated, and it will be stressful at times. But how you'll get there is simple. It starts with these three words: Be an expert.

My multi-cultural experience at Y-Camp, 1953.
I'm sitting at the bottom, right.

My father, Arnold, showing off the features of his
sewing machine: "Look, no hands, even a child can do this!"

Our wedding reception, 1970, Buffalo, New York.

My baby shower where I'm pregnant with Nicole, 1972.

Saeed celebrates the grand opening of Nourmand and Associates, 1976.

Nicole (7) and Howard (3), and
my hairdo inspired by Charlie's Angels.

My three shining diamonds: Howard (6), Nicole (6), and Michael (7).
If a mother's place is in the home, why am I at tap, jazz, ballet,
basketball, piano, madrigals, and baseball with the car running?

Family photo (from left to right): Howard, Myra, Saeed, and Michael.

The Nourmand Legacy continues with Michael taking on the family business.

What Brings You Here?

When I started out, I was a newly licensed broker who had *never* before sold a piece of property. And it had been years since I had worked full time at all. I had prior sales experience, but selling waterless cookware to brides as a 22-year-old was one thing—multi-million-dollar homes was another. Now that I was a real estate salesperson, I had to figure out where to begin.

Perhaps you've decided to become a real estate agent after working in a completely unrelated field. At this point, you may be asking yourself, "Is this the right profession for me?"

For instance, you may have been an actor or schoolteacher, and now you've decided to become a full-time broker. Or you may have relocated—you were working in another area, maybe even another state, and you've left your contacts behind. Perhaps you've been a full-time homemaker, but now that your kids are grown, you want to start a real estate career. Or perhaps you've recently divorced or lost a spouse and have decided to become a real estate agent.

Whatever your circumstances, you know that you're capable and motivated. But you may not have a client list, connections, or database that will bring you business right away.

At the same time, if you think hard about whom you know, you may be pleasantly surprised. You may already have a contact list comprising of family members, friends, and acquaintances.

In 1988, I took the exam to become a real estate broker. When I look back, passing the test was the easy part. The real work involved creating a client list, becoming an expert in my area, and creating contacts within the community. Just like me, you may not have any experience selling homes, and you may not have an extensive client base—but don't let this discourage you. In this chapter, I'll share what experience has taught me about long-term success in real estate.

WHY MOTHERHOOD WAS GOOD FOR BUSINESS

Once my first child, Nicole, was born, I quit my job to be a full-time mother. Afterwards, when my sons Howard and Michael were born, life became even busier. Our children were the Number 1 priority for my husband and me. Saeed was building the business, which allowed me to commit all of my time to being with our children. Between swimming, dancing, soccer, school plays, orchestra, and gymnastics, all three kids were active all day. This meant that I was in charge of coordinating their schedules, arranging for transportation, and attending school functions.

When my children were older, Saeed encouraged me to begin a career in real estate. Once I plunged into the profession, I asked myself questions like, "Who will make up my contact list?" and "Who would be interested in buying a home from me?"

At first, those around me had their doubts about whether I would succeed as a real estate broker. They thought that I was entering this profession on a whim, where my commitment would be no greater than had I decided to take up knitting or salsa dancing. After all, almost everyone around me knew me as Myra Nourmand: mother, wife, and social butterfly. Adding real estate broker to the list was new.

I had my own misgivings as well. But I didn't allow the uncertainty to stop me. I was determined to build my business and accomplish my goals, which reflects the optimistic outlook that I've always had.

My lifelong philosophy is that people always get their share of good or bad luck: Misfortune strikes even the luckiest, and the silver lining surrounds even the darkest cloud. When you can turn a tough situation into something positive, you know that you'll adapt to life's experiences with confidence.

Suddenly, the contact list that I thought was non-existent became full of possibilities. I realized that I had strong connections to parents within my community. With other moms and dads, we had spent years attending practices and rehearsals, shared parenthood stories, and watched competitions and performances. Through our time together, we had grown to trust and count on each other and ask one another for help when urgent matters arose. I began contacting these friends. Thus, my client list started with individuals whom I knew long before I decided to become a broker.

EVERYONE WANTS SOMETHING FOR NOTHING

Beverly Hills has the reputation of being home to the world's rich and famous. In fact, it could be the most high-profile place to live in the world. So what do you think my colleagues said when I told them that I planned to build my business by giving away chocolate purchased from a school fundraiser?

What I heard was, "Are you sure about this?" And their expressions told me, "What are you thinking?" But despite the skeptics, I went ahead and bought cases of candy at my son's school. My closets swelled with boxes and boxes of chocolates. In fact, I made my son the top-producing candy seller at his school. The plan was a success. In order to explain why, let me take you from Beverly Hills back to my roots in Buffalo, New York.

In high school, I took a job selling makeup at a fancy department store. Working there, with clientele who had lots of money and spent it on expensive products, made me realize that the high end of the market was where I could excel.

I stood behind the glass counter and advised older women on how to look younger and more beautiful. I learned that people believe what they want to. If they think that opening up an expensive bottle of skin cream will make them look younger, they'll make the purchase.

The customers who frequented my makeup counter were inspired by my youthful skin, which convinced them that the cheap products sold at the drug store were useless. What they didn't realize was that my skin looked youthful because it was—I was only 16 after all—and that I was using the inexpensive products sold in the local drug store.

Next, I worked as a telemarketer. I was responsible for arranging appointments with prospective customers and the sales staff, who were selling fire alarms. The tricky part was that I was never allowed to mention fire alarms in my telephone pitch. Instead, I called individuals at home and asked, "Ma'am would you be interested in learning more about fire safety?"

In order to bring in customers, I offered incentives. For example, if I was calling during the Thanksgiving Holiday, I offered a free turkey. Or if it was Christmas, I offered a free pie cutter.

I learned that people were motivated to act when offered something free, even if it was just a pie cutter. Later, to my surprise, my manager told me that I was one of the few telemarketers who consistently filled up the schedules of all the salesmen.

While in college in Buffalo, I saw an ad on campus that read, "College Students: Earn $500 a week from selling lifetime waterless cookware." That was a lot of money, and the ad piqued my interest.

Once hired, I attended bridal fairs, set up booths at shopping malls, and met brides-to-be in their homes. At the time, I was also engaged to marry Saeed. Therefore, my customers and I had something in common. The job taught me that if I surrounded myself with people with similar experiences, I was able to relate to them better, understand their needs, and earn their trust.

The job reminded me of watching my father work. Successfully selling sewing machines allowed him to earn enough money to buy a furniture store. He intentionally bought a business in a Polish neighborhood so that he could relate to his customers' culture and language. Through him, I realized that the key to successful sales was to find my niche.

When I spoke with brides-to-be, I told them that in addition to the cookware, they could pick their own flatware, stemware, and china, and that by the time they were married, they would have a complete set. Within a short period of time, I was selling five sets of cookware per week.

My supervisor was astonished. This was another case of "what you don't know might help you." Because no one had told me differently, I assumed that after every night of work, I was supposed to have sold a set of cookware. That's why I didn't consider it an option to finish the day without a sale. To my amusement, he shared that I was selling more cookware in a week than most of his sales staff did in a month, which made me their top salesperson.

Once I embarked on a real estate career in Beverly Hills, I took these valuable lessons with me. As I mentioned previously, many thought it was a silly idea to buy school fundraiser chocolate and give it away as gifts. This was Beverly Hills, not Buffalo, after all. Who in 90210 would want something so trivial?

It turned out to be a great way to meet people. A phone call starting with, "Hello Julie, I just bought some chocolate to raise money for Michael's school. Can I bring you a gift?" opened many doors for me. I would arrive at Julie's home, and we would catch up with family news. This provided an ideal way to introduce my new career endeavor.

My school fundraising days are now over, but the philosophy hasn't changed: *Giving to others is one of the easiest ways to create opportunity.* I can't emphasize enough how important this will be to your career.

REAL ESTATE TIPS YOUR MOM WOULD BE PROUD OF

I love children. My kids—Nicole, Howard, and Michael— are the three biggest blessings in my life. And now that they have children of their own, I once again have little ones running around the house. If I had to sum up in one word what being a mother and grandmother has taught me, it would be PATIENCE.

Raising three children has taught me how to take care of my clients who are parents of little ones. For example, if I'm driving a client to a listing and she has children, I know how to prepare. As a mother myself, I understand how distracting children can be. As a real estate broker, I realize how important it is that my client is able to commit her full attention to what could be her future home. So before the meeting, I stock my purse with crayons, coloring books, and small refreshments like cheese, crackers, and fruit.

It always warms my heart when my clients' children see me and say something like, "Hi Myra, do you have any treats for me?" As you can imagine, many of these kids have every type of toy and food under the sun. But they still look forward to receiving a simple surprise. Once we arrive at the listing, the children are already occupied with a coloring book or some crackers, and their parents are able to focus on finding their home.

YOUR JOURNEY STARTS WITH A CLIENT IN YOUR CAR

Often, you'll spend an entire afternoon with a client. You may have four homes lined up to see, which means that you will spend the next few hours together. Many real estate agents prefer driving separately to listings, but unless your clients choose to do differently, I suggest that you take them in your car.

Having time together gives you and your clients a chance to talk. You'll get to know them better and understand what they are looking to buy. Simple gestures—like offering pretzels, bottled water, and other light snacks—go a long way toward making your clients comfortable and building a relationship with them.

TIPS TO MAKE WORK FUN

When you read stories about successful people in any industry, you'll discover that they all share a passion for their work while having fun in the process. What does having fun mean? This is different for every profession.

In real estate, one of the most enjoyable aspects is working with interesting people. Your clients could be CEOs, actors, lawyers, or doctors. You'll constantly meet people with fascinating lives. Having fun in real estate involves making the most out of the relationships you create.

For instance, giving away chocolates to my friends and providing treats for children were simple and fun ways to leave a lasting impression on my clients. The following are three other suggestions.

First, get to know your client. News is an easy way to start conversation. I read the *Los Angeles Times* every morning. I keep up with current events and always have something to discuss when I'm driving my clients to a listing.

Look through each section of the paper: world news, business, food, health, or entertainment. Then start a conversation with something like, "Hey, did you see the latest Tom Hanks film? It got great reviews in the *Times*." Or, "I recently read an article about a new Mediterranean restaurant. Have you heard of it?" From these conversations, you may learn that your client enjoys films or fell in love with hummus during a recent trip to Greece.

Secondly, remind yourself to continually smile. It has a powerful effect on you and those around you. The opposite is true as well. Do you know people who consistently have frowns on their faces? They appear as if their lives are full of tragedy or that they are unhappy with life. It's difficult to be around these people because they manage to sap the energy out of you.

On the other hand, there are individuals who seem to always have smiles on their faces, greet you, and treat you warmly. These individuals project confidence and optimism. If you're lucky enough to be around successful, positive people like these, they are great sources for picking up tips. Watch what they do and emulate them. Remember, you're fortunate to be in a profession where the sky is the limit to your success.

Finally, create an environment that encourages you to feel happy, where you can't help but smile. For instance, I have nicknames that I give the homes around my neighborhood. This light-hearted practice always makes me smile.

Most homes throughout Beverly Hills, Bel Air, Brentwood, and Holmby Hills are beautifully maintained and could easily appear on the cover of *Architectural Digest*, while others' claim to fame is their over-the-top architecture or overgrown landscaping.

There is one house that I call Caesar's Palace. The property is located on a huge lot, and the front yard extends far beyond the main house. The residents have taken advantage of their expansive front yard by placing plaster statues on the lawn. Twelve life-size sculptures of biblical figures such as David and icons like Caesar greet visitors just like they do at the famous casino in Las Vegas.

Homes nearby are tough to sell because buyers balk at the idea of living next to something that could belong on the Vegas Strip. Another home that was a hard sell had a miniature Statue of Liberty on the front lawn. When I asked the owner why he had Lady Liberty greeting guests, he said that it reminded his wife of her New York roots. I told the story to the buyer, and this actually led him to leave the symbol of freedom on the lawn once he moved in. So much for "Give me your tired, your poor, your huddled masses..."

There is another home that I call Taco Bell. Its architecture is a combination of Mediterranean and Meximelt. Nicknaming houses has two benefits. First, it's an amusing way to point out a home's distinct features. Secondly, it makes it easier for your clients to recall the home later. "I really like the house that was close to the Taco Bell one," is something that I'll hear my client tell me.

GOOD REAL ESTATE BROKERS ARE GOOD TEACHERS

As a successful real estate broker, your job is to educate your clients. Not only are you teaching them about the service you provide, but you're also giving them information that will help them make the best decision.

For example, I had a client who determined that he wanted to spend $6 million on his next home. He wanted to live in the Holmby Hills area of Los Angeles, and he was looking for a big lot with a view of the city. Based on my knowledge of the area, I determined that $6 million would not buy a home that met his specifications.

When I shared this information with him, he became obstinate. "My wife and I refuse to spend a penny more than $6 million," I recall him telling me. Although I knew this wouldn't be possible, based on current market conditions where he wanted to buy, I realized that he needed to see this for himself.

I suggested that we spend the afternoon looking at homes in Holmby Hills. We met, and I drove him to several properties that I had sold in the neighborhood. Many of the listings were similar to what he was looking for, but all were valued at more than $6 million. After seeing the properties, I invited him to my home where we could discuss what we had observed that day.

Before I left for work that morning, I prepared a plate of fresh fruit, as I knew that my client and I would de-brief afterwards back at my home. We sat in my living room, and I listened to him discuss the day's events.

"$6 million was my absolute spending limit, but after you showed me around today, I realize that I need to reconsider," he told me. He later thanked me for educating him about the neighborhood and providing him with the information he needed to change his plans. In the end, he recognized he would have to either spend more than he had initially budgeted or rethink the kind of property he wanted to purchase.

This example illustrates that as a broker, your job is to provide your clients with information that will allow them to make the best possible choice. To do this successfully, you have to be sensitive to their needs. This means that you express your opinions in a way that shows that they are your Number 1 priority and that you value their time.

In the case of the client I just described, what convinced him to think twice about his plans was my knowledge of the area where he sought to live. In order for you to earn your clients' respect, and for them to trust your opinion, you must have extensive knowledge of the community you serve. I'll explain what this involves in Chapter 3. For now, you must know your inventory, which means that you have done exhaustive research about homes in the area you serve.

TRUST YOUR CONNECTIONS AND ENJOY THE JOURNEY

When I started my career, I didn't have any real estate experience. What I did have were friends and acquaintances whose children were friends with my children. And these moms and dads all lived in homes.

Everyone has friends and acquaintances. In your case, you may not be a full-time mother. Perhaps you're in your 60s and have many friends who are selling their homes. They seek to scale down and want the freedom of living in a condominium instead of a detached house. Or you may be an artist with strong connections within the creative community.

Regardless of whom you know, opportunity awaits you. Your goal is to figure out your niche. We all know many people; let those around you know what you do. Then share with them how you can help them find their dream homes.

Throughout the process, always remember to love your work. If you're a passionate and skilled professional, success tends to follow. So revel in the journey by having fun. Encourage friendly conversation with your clients or create silly names for properties within your neighborhood. Do whatever you can to make your job something that you enjoy every day.

Lastly, remember to be an expert and share your knowledge with your clients. Once they realize how much you know and what a consummate professional you are, you've moved one significant step toward having a client for life. In the next chapter, I'll share the Four E's of Success that will form the foundation of your business.

Are You Ready to Be a Sales Superstar?

Success in this business is possible for anyone who is willing to put in the long hours. When I first started, I spent countless time on the phone, consumed hours researching my community, and worked tirelessly to expand my contact list. Unfortunately, I wasted a lot of time because I navigated my way through trial and error.

In this chapter, I'll share the lessons I've learned throughout my career. By following my tips, you'll avoid some headaches, and you'll move ahead of your competition.

The following are the Four E's of Success, which form the foundation of my business. Adopt them, and they'll be the driving force behind your success.

1. **Effort:** Work hard and remain positive.
2. **Expertise:** Tirelessly research your community.
3. **Ethics:** Uphold the highest professional standards and follow the Golden Rule.
4. **Enthusiasm:** Know that you're the best one to serve your clients and be willing to shamelessly express it.

"E" NUMBER 1: EFFORT

There is one guiding principal that you must learn to accept: Every sale will have a glitch. Whether it's a bad inspection or an unreasonable broker on the other end of the deal, you must be prepared to adjust to obstacles that arise. Too many in this industry give up when success is around the corner. They let negative thoughts interfere with closing the deal.

Your flexibility will allow you to see a solution to every problem rather than view setbacks as insurmountable deal-breakers. When approached by positive thinking, you'll realize that the challenges you face are simply part of the transaction process.

In addition, you have to be prepared to work through the ups and downs of the real estate market. For instance, when the market is hot, the deals seem to fall into your lap out of nowhere. Your career is off to a good start, and you enjoy your work immensely. That's great. But once the market is in a slump, you'll see how tough you really are.

During a slow period, your listings are on the MLS (Multiple Listing Service) longer than you believe you can bear. Your clients are frustrated because no one is interested in their home, and they are afraid of losing money on the sale. Your phone isn't ringing, and bad news about real estate seems to appear everywhere you look. It's these difficult times that separate the agents who viewed real estate as a fast way to earn money from those who have long-term career plans.

After you've been in the business a few years, you'll understand why adversity is your friend. When you work harder, push yourself, and dig deeper to find gold, you learn more about the business.

In the beginning, I used to feel anxious when I considered how many other brokers I was competing against. But not anymore. When the real estate market is strong, everyone from the attorney to his accountant is an agent. If you wait long enough, however, you'll see those same professionals, who became top producers as a result of a couple of deals they did almost nothing to get, drop out of the business once the market takes a dive.

As tough as it can be during a dry spell, you've got to continually believe that things will turn around. If it's your first time in a slump, welcome to the club. It'll require a leap of faith to believe that business will improve. Trust me on this one. Unless you're working in an area that people can't wait to leave, the skills you learn during lean times will benefit you immensely once the market improves. Even in places that insurance companies insist are risky areas in which to live, you'll still find numerous buyers who are willing to take the gamble and buy the property.

Malibu, for example, is home to the world's rich and famous. It is also documented as an area at risk for landslides, floods, fire, earthquakes, and tsunamis. In fact, Malibu is one of the only parts of the country that is jeopardized by all five of these major threats from Mother Nature.

A flash fire will devastate a hillside in Malibu, turning some of the world's most expensive homes into ash. A landslide will rip apart an architectural masterpiece. But after the initial shock, what happens? Within months, new buyers purchase properties or homeowners rebuild despite the threats that are stated on their insurance policies.

My point is that for every negative belief, there is a positive one that can take its place. Don't let fear get in the way of accomplishing your goals. You can certainly find any number of reasons why you won't make it in this business: natural disasters, economic slumps, and personal weaknesses. Despite these limitations, however, countless individuals are making a living and reaching their professional goals every day. How do they do this? They remain upbeat, create a supportive environment, and put in the effort.

"E" NUMBER 2: EXPERTISE

All of the four E's are important, as without one, the other three would collapse. But if I had to pick the most significant, it would be this one. In fact, it's so important that you'll read an entire chapter on expert status later. For now, I'll explain why being an expert is so important.

Ask me about any neighborhood in Beverly Hills, Holmby Hills, and Bel Air, and I'll be able to tell you its strengths and weaknesses. I can also tell you about the history of countless homes: Who has lived where, what renovations have been made, the price the home has sold for, and its sales history.

You must be able to do the same where you work, which means that *you must know your inventory*. When a prospect calls and asks how far the home is from an elementary school, you should not only tell him the distance but also details about the school: its reputation, its strengths, and how it measures up to other schools within the community.

You should also be able to answer the following questions without having to say, "I'll get back to you about that."

- What are the comparable homes worth?
- Is the home that they're looking at a good deal?

- Do the renovations that were made five years ago justify the listing's price?
- Why is the home's price significantly higher than the one next to it?

This information isn't on the MLS, and it's not something that a web site will describe. Instead, it comes from the countless hours you've invested attending open houses, talking to residents, and researching listings.

Expert status will separate you from your colleagues. It's what will keep your prospects on the phone asking more questions, what will encourage them to set up a meeting with you, and—most importantly—what will close the deal.

"E" NUMBER 3: ETHICS

A few years ago, I was hosting an open house in Bel Air— one of the most prestigious neighborhoods in Los Angeles. The sellers listed the home for $12 million, and the opulent estate was worth every penny.

It was the end of the day, and I was preparing to take my signs down and draw the curtains shut. In the distance, I heard the rumble of a car. I looked out the picture window and saw a clunker that seemed more Beverly Hillbilly than Bel Air.

The car made its way around the circular driveway and stopped at the front door. Out stepped an elderly man and his companion, a small woman with a giant wig and a vinyl skirt that reflected the afternoon sun. The couple ambled up the stairs, and I opened the door.

"May I help you?" I asked, concerned that I wouldn't be able to give them directions to the nearest swap meet.

"Yes. My girlfriend and I were driving through the neighborhood, and we stumbled onto your house. Can we have a look?" he asked.

I obliged, and they entered the foyer. "What kind of home are you looking for?" I asked, doubtful that I could help them.

"Well, I just turned 80, and I'm looking to move into a new neighborhood. My girlfriend and I are planning to get married," he said. He put his arm around the plastic-coated woman and drew her near his body. "Doris is beautiful, isn't she? You wouldn't believe that she just turned 68."

I nodded, wishing to cut the real estate meeting short to address more pressing matters, such as finding Doris a hairpiece that fit and a dress free from waterproof fabric. Besides, there was no way this couple could afford a $12 million home, I thought to myself.

I showed the two around, and after a cursory tour, they loaded themselves in the car and left in a cloud of blue smoke. I didn't bother taking their contact information and neglected to provide them a business card.

Two weeks later, a young, newly licensed agent was elated to have landed a coup in his brief career. Michael explained the deal he had just closed. He was doing floor time when he took a call from an elderly man. Once he revealed more information about his buyer—his beat up car and his garishly dressed girlfriend—the connection was unmistakable. This was the man who appeared at my $12 million listing on that Saturday afternoon.

The elderly gentleman, whom I assumed couldn't possibly afford to buy my seller's Bel Air mansion, had spent his career as an accountant buying real estate and had just sold his collection of apartment buildings. The buyer ended up paying all cash for a $9 million home near the one where we met two weeks earlier. It was a humbling experience that I've never forgotten.

To avoid making the same mistake, insist on providing the same high-level of service to everyone. Who knows if the starving writer whom you assume is a waste of time will turn around and become the next executive producer of a hit show on TV or if the young woman you're talking to will be promoted to CFO. You never know how the kindness you've extended toward the home's housekeeper will benefit you later. Perhaps she's a trusted member of the family, and her opinion of you will mean that a homeowner will select you as her agent.

When you treat everyone well, they'll remember. In real estate, it's not about one deal. You must keep your focus on creating long-term relationships that will last you your entire career.

In addition, working ethically means upholding the regulations established by your local Board of Realtors. Sadly, the real estate industry is notorious for high turn-around and disciplinary action against Realtors. To avoid this, commit to adhering to the highest ethical standards. Disclose any information that you know about listings regardless of how it may affect the deal.

Remember, your reputation is only as good as your last transaction. If you cut corners and get sloppy, it'll take years to rebuild the trust that you've lost.

Lastly, treat your clients and colleagues the way you want to be treated. Be on time to appointments. Phone ahead if this isn't possible. Most agents will understand if your current listing appointment has run long, making you late to theirs.

Return phone calls promptly. Work tirelessly to follow-up, even if it means you're cutting into your vacation. I once interrupted my trip in Europe to make an important conference call between my client, his attorney, and his business manager, all three of whom were in Los Angeles.

In order for me to be on time for our 11:00 a.m. appointment in LA, I remained awake until 2:00 a.m. in Amsterdam. I refused to go to bed before the conference call because I was afraid I might miss the meeting. It doesn't happen all the time, but actions like these are sometimes necessary to close the deal.

"E" NUMBER 4: ENTHUSIASM

Your clients are expecting you to represent them in one of the biggest investments of their lives. The more you can project enthusiasm and confidence, which signifies an unwavering ability to take care of their needs, the more they'll rely on you and not question your approach.

By confidence, I don't mean haughtiness or arrogance. Although it works for some agents, many people are put off by brokers whose egos are bigger than the backyard of a Holmby Hills estate. More importantly, a false sense of pride has the potential to kill a deal. Brokers who let their egos get in the way often ruin a sale. They're too busy trying to be right and stubbornly hold onto their position, even if it means putting the transaction at risk.

When you've done your homework, your enthusiasm will follow. After you've fulfilled everything in the Expertise section, you can answer your clients' questions with confidence. When you speak with a broker and he presents you with information that is inaccurate, you can tactfully correct his error. Enthusiasm that comes from being an expert is what will be one of the defining characteristics of your career. It's what will establish you as the source of information for your clients and colleagues.

Enthusiasm also means that you're prepared to walk away when circumstances may put your reputation at risk. No deal, as important as it may seem, is worth diminishing your impeccable track record.

Be passionate about the homes you sell. You're in the business of providing one of the most important resources to your clients—their homes. Through real estate, you're improving lives, making your clients money, and creating relationships that will last your entire lifetime.

FOLLOW THE YELLOW BRICK ROAD AND
YOU'LL FIND THE POT-OF-GOLD UNDER THE RAINBOW

The Four E's of Real Estate, **Effort, Expertise, Ethics, and Enthusiasm**, will form the foundation of your career. As simple as they seem, these four qualities separate the seasonal agent—the one who works when it's easy—from brokers who achieve long-term success.

Effort requires tenacity, a positive outlook, and a tireless investment of time and energy. Real estate is fun *and* hard work. I think you'll agree that enjoying yourself while working hard is a fulfilling way to spend your workday.

Expertise will require an immense amount of your time. It means that you'll be in regular communication with your colleagues, you'll attend open houses throughout the week, and you'll know so much about your community that you can immediately answer almost any question about it.

Ethics is the Golden Rule: Do unto others as you would have done unto you. It means avoiding costly mistakes by treating others with respect and always disclosing information about listings, even when it means that you may lose business. Remember, one dishonest move on your part can ruin a reputation that you've taken years to build.

Enthusiasm comes as a result of the time you've invested in the other three E's of real estate. You've paid your dues through diligent work, you're the expert in your community, and you hold yourself to the highest ethical standards. Now it's time to reap the rewards by holding your head high and letting your clients know that their decision to work with you will benefit them immensely.

Now you're ready to explore how you can become the most sought-after source of real estate information in your community.

Expert Status is the Fast Track to Success

It takes 20 years to build a reputation and five minutes to ruin it. If you think about that, you'll do things differently.

—*Warren Buffet*

In the previous chapter, I discussed the Four E's of Real Estate: **Effort, Expertise, Ethics, and Enthusiasm**. In this chapter, I'll expand on the second E: Expertise. Once you're an expert in your area, people will come to you.

SPECIALIZED KNOWLEDGE MATTERS

I met a client who contacted me about a listing he saw online. The house met all of his criteria: It was in a desirable part of the city, was close to his office, and had the right square footage. He phoned me, and he was ready to buy. Once he told me where the home was, I broke the news to him—the listing was right next to a freeway. Needless to say, he was disappointed. He certainly had no intention of living by an LA highway and greatly appreciated the information.

In his case, the photos online looked appealing, but none of them revealed that the house was next to the 10 Freeway.

This kind of information is something that only an expert agent would recognize right away.

In another instance, I was representing a Hollywood Studio executive. From the beginning, Jeff and his wife had a clear vision of what they planned to buy. They sought a Spanish-style home with spectacular views situated on a large lot. The two had a significant amount of money to invest and were willing to wait until they found their dream home.

Over the course of several months, I looked for a listing that would meet their requirements. After almost a year, I received a tip about a home that was for sale but not yet on the market. I drove to the listing right away. After walking through it, I knew that it was precisely what the couple wanted. I phoned my client right away.

"Colleen, I've found what you've been looking for. It's not listed yet, so you've gotta come see it right now," I recall telling her.

"Tell me about it." she said.

"It's in the best part of Santa Monica and has a view that'll take your breath away. It's a hot property, so bring your checkbook," I said.

Colleen arrived at the listing and found her dream home—the Spanish architecture, the view of the Brentwood golf course, the tennis court, pool, and landscaping all met her requirements. She phoned her husband. He saw the listing the same day and agreed that it was the home that he and his wife had been dreaming to buy.

They needed to act fast. The house would attract much attention once it appeared on the MLS. To avoid competition, I suggested that Jeff make an all-cash offer and buy the home at its full list price. He agreed. We submitted a clean offer that made it clear that we wanted the house. The seller accepted, and the home went into escrow.

I set up an inspection with one of the most well-respected contracting companies in the city. I met the inspector and waited as he completed a thorough assessment of the home's condition.

Afterwards, his expression told me that he didn't like what he saw.

"Myra, you have to walk away from this deal," he said.

"Why?" I asked.

"This is a hollow clay tile structure. It's not safe."

"But I've worked with plenty of hollow clay homes. What's wrong with this one?" I asked.

"This area is earthquake prone. I can't give my seal of approval because it's not wood framed," he said.

Hollow clay tile was cutting-edge construction when the historic house was built, a time before multiple-zone climate control. The insulation that hollow clay tile homes provided was superior to that of other construction methods. In addition, these homes were resistant to fire. Unfortunately, many did not stand up to earthquakes because the tile didn't reinforce the home as effectively as a wood frame.

I shared the bad news with my clients. The couple had their hearts set on buying this home, but they were now advised to back out of the purchase and start the home search all over again.

After the inspection, I phoned my husband, Saeed, and told him about the inspector's report. I recall his response after I expressed my disappointment.

"Is that it?" he asked.

"What do you mean? The inspector told me to look for another home."

"Tell your clients not to worry. I'm going to call someone."

"Who?" I asked.

"Remember when we wanted to buy the Hollywood Athletic Club? And remember what the inspectors said about that?"

His question called to mind what happened. The inspectors noted the building would need extensive structural reinforcement because it was a hollow clay tile building. Unfortunately, any such changes would alter the building's appearance. Saeed refused to ruin the exterior of the historic building and believed that there had to be a way to make the structure safe while preserving its original character.

Saeed did his research and contacted a renowned authority on un-reinforced masonry buildings. Ken was a busy man whose schedule was filled with conferences, publishing, and consulting. His expertise was known throughout the architectural community.

Working together, Saeed and Ken were able to develop a plan to reinforce the Hollywood Athletic Club while maintaining its distinctive exterior. Through their collaboration, Ken and Saeed became friends.

My husband told me that he would ask Ken to inspect the Santa Monica home. I phoned my clients and shared the good news with them. The next week, Saeed picked up the architect from his Pasadena home—Ken typically commuted by bicycle—and they drove to the listing. They spent the next couple of hours walking through the interior, checking the attic, and crawling under the home itself.

Ken gave the property a clean bill of health. He informed us that the original architect of the historic property had mastered the art of hollow clay tile homes. He was a man who was ahead of his time and knew the potential weaknesses of the technology. Therefore, unlike many un-reinforced concrete buildings, this one was safe.

He *did* add that in order to make the home as solid as any wood frame structure in the neighborhood, minor changes would be necessary, but these corrections were simple to implement.

Ken then contacted the original inspector and convinced him to retract his original assessment. This not only gave Jeff and Colleen peace of mind but in the future would also allow them to sell their home without any problems. As a result of Ken's seal of approval, my clients' dream home became a reality.

EXPERT STATUS GOES BEYOND THE WORLD WIDE WEB

When the Internet became a common resource for information, many thought that the real estate agent's exclusive hold on information would be weakened. After all, if the public could access the MLS, research properties, and find out about neighborhoods online, why would they need an agent?

What happened, however, was the opposite: The role of the real estate agent became more important than ever. But to be successful today, you must have more information and more knowledge than your clients do. For instance, a colleague of yours will tell you that his client is selling his home. He shares this with you before the listing appears on the MLS. Now you have an inside scoop that your clients don't—regardless of their ability to access properties online.

In other instances, your clients will seek your advice about the community where they plan to move. And because neighborhoods change from street to street, you'll have information that no web site will. For example, on one block you may find homes with impeccably manicured lawns and large estates, while on the next one, there will be smaller homes that are not as meticulously maintained. Your clients may not be aware of these differences and ask you for help.

So how do you stand out when the market is saturated with brokers who claim that they're the best and most successful?

Allow me to share an analogy. When a customer walks into an electronics store to purchase a flat screen TV, his options are enormous. He has a wide range of sets made from companies such as Sony, Panasonic, and Toshiba. What these manufacturers offer are high-quality products that are quite similar to one another.

How do most consumers make their final choice? They base their purchases on the advice of a skilled salesperson. The professional who has the most product knowledge and effective communication skills will convince a buyer to invest in a particular television—even one he may not have purchased otherwise.

Real estate is the same. When you're a broker, your job is to provide your clients with the most information possible. You'll stand out by knowing more about homes than anyone else and by having more insight into the local market you serve.

DO YOUR HOMEWORK

A broker will phone me and ask, "Hi Myra, I saw your listing on Lincoln. Could you tell me how many bedrooms it has?" There is little excuse for a broker to ask basic questions like this. Professionals who won't even log on to the MLS to find out how many bedrooms a listing has are unlikely to be disciplined and driven to succeed in this business.

In today's ultra-competitive world of real estate, where commissions are higher than they have ever been, you have to work harder and know more than your competitors like never before. At first, you may have beginner's luck and sell a listing to a family member—such as a cousin or uncle—but making real estate a lifelong career takes more than just good fortune. It requires a tremendous amount of work.

TECHNOLOGY HAS MADE YOUR JOB EASIER...*SOMEWHAT*

All the high-tech tools that we rely on—PDAs, mobile phones, laptops, and navigation systems—are both blessings and curses. They have made our jobs easier, but keeping up with the latest technology is a time-consuming endeavor in itself. Not only that, but today, work follows you anywhere you go.

Twenty years ago, none of this information-based gear was widely available. Although there were disadvantages to working without these modern conveniences, successful brokers learned the importance of communication and how to depend on their colleagues.

Early in my career, I found many listings by driving around the neighborhood and spotting "For Sale" signs on front lawns. In the event that I saw a new home for sale, I would jot down the number that appeared at the bottom of the sign, get to the nearest payphone, and call the broker.

Often, the pay phone was my communication hub. If I was late for a showing, I gathered the change in my pocket and phoned the broker to let him know. If I needed to speak with a client about a hot property that I just saw, I stopped at the nearest phone booth. I would call over and over until someone picked up because there was no voicemail.

Driving up and down the streets of Beverly Hills, Brentwood, and Holmby Hills was an important part of my workday. I was perpetually on the look-out for new listings. I could be driving my daughter to a dance lesson and suddenly see a "For Sale" sign that had just been planted on a front lawn. Before arriving at rehearsal, I would pull off the road and make a quick phone call to the listing agent.

Communicating with colleagues and friends within the neighborhood was another way to receive the latest real estate news. Brokers had to stay on top of what was happening within the community in order to act fast when a client needed help.

For example, when I heard about a recent divorce, I knew that it meant a home would most likely be listed for sale. In addition to marriage break-ups, I kept track of who lived where, who was getting married, who recently passed away, and who had a serious illness. I also regularly met with my colleagues, and we would share what we had for sale.

Although the landscape has changed, and now I simply press "send" on my mobile phone or e-mail a client, the fundamentals of the business haven't. No amount of technology can substitute seeing a home in person, creating lasting relationships with residents, and regularly communicating with colleagues and clients.

LESSONS THAT WILL MAKE YOU AN EXPERT

As the Dickens classic begins, "It was the best of times, it was the worst of times." Years ago, when you left the office, work didn't follow. Today, work can go wherever you go—a client is just a text message or e-mail away. Technological advances and the large number of people entering the real estate profession have transformed the industry.

In many ways, high-tech gear has made your job easier. Cell phones mean that you can contact your clients almost anywhere, and faxes allow you to send and receive contracts without having to drive across town for a signature. But the same technology that has made your job easier is available to your clients as well.

This means that you have to work harder and smarter than ever before. You have to show your clients that you have information that they don't.

In addition, the number of brokerages, brokers, and agents has reached an all-time high. In fact, just a few years ago in Beverly Hills, companies with names like Coldwell Banker, Sotheby's, Keller-Williams, and RE/MAX didn't exist.

Instead, most people identified a real estate brokerage by the name of its owner, who was well-known within the community. Today, the larger offices often employ hundreds of agents, which makes competition fierce. Therefore, to stand out from the countless other agents and brokers within your community, you must commit a tremendous amount of energy into your business.

THE EARLY BIRD CATCHES THE WORM

One of the most significant ways that you'll earn respect from your prospects and clients is by having more information about listings than anyone else. There are two simple ways to do this.

FIRST, PREVIEW LISTINGS BEFORE THE TUESDAY CARAVAN.

When most brokers want to see the latest listing, they'll wait for a home to appear on the MLS. Then they'll tour the home during a weekly caravan. But why wait for business to come to you?

Instead, once you drive by the "For Sale" sign or see the listing on the MLS, act quickly. Go through your client list and figure out who would be likely to purchase the home.

Now it's time to phone the listing agent and set up an appointment. And don't wait for the Tuesday caravan. By planning ahead, you're taking charge of your business. As a result, you may close a deal before the home is even on the MLS.

SECOND, CONSIDER YOUR COLLEAGUES YOUR FRIENDS.

Like I shared earlier, in the days before mobile phones and the Internet, I learned about many listings through my colleagues. I contacted them on a regular basis, and we would exchange information. Through this experience, I learned that contrary to what many say, your colleagues aren't your enemies. In fact, it's important to maintain good relations with your fellow brokers because they can help make deals happen. When you respect one another and share information with each other, your business will benefit.

BEING AN EXPERT MEANS
THAT YOU'RE AHEAD OF THE GAME

I'll have a client tell me, "Myra, I want to buy a contemporary home."

So far so good. Next I'll ask, "Where do you want to live?"

"Brentwood," he'll answer.

For most of you, this scenario sounds simple enough. But if you're a real estate agent who has worked in Brentwood and consider yourself an expert in this part of LA, you realize how difficult it will be to fulfill this buyer's request.

In your case, you can name a city that you know and set up a similar scenario. To make an exaggerated case, consider a client who is looking to raise horses in an urban center. To succeed in real estate, you must know your neighborhood better than anyone else.

In order to stand out from your competitors, you must know your inventory and know your comparables.

KNOW YOUR INVENTORY BY KICKING THE TIRES

The example that I shared earlier, where the broker phoned me to ask how many bedrooms my listing had, points to how little many of your colleagues know about what is in their market. The broker who contacted me didn't thoroughly research it online or attend one of my open houses. There is little excuse for agents not to know basic details such as square footage, lot size, bedrooms and bathrooms, and architectural style. If an agent doesn't have this information, then he hasn't done his homework.

The easiest way to have a grasp of your inventory is by "kicking the tires," which means attending open houses and weekly caravans and taking note of what is selling in the neighborhood. During an open house, talk to the listing agent and learn more about the property and the seller.

In addition, drive around your neighborhood. Notice details about the community that you may have otherwise overlooked. Are there any parks nearby? Are there any homes that stand out from the rest? Are there certain streets that attract more traffic than others? Armed with this information, you'll be able to answer your clients' questions and address their concerns.

KNOW YOUR COMPARABLES: WHAT JUSTIFIES THE LIST PRICE?

When you're representing your clients in a sale or purchase of a home, extensive knowledge of comparables is key. What makes an accurate comparable? To give a simple illustration, you want to compare apples to apples and oranges to oranges. In other words, how much did the house up the street last sell for, and what was it like compared to others?

For example, let's say that you're planning to buy jewelry. When you're comparing precious stones, you want the jeweler to match up minerals of similar qualities, facets, and cuts. In the case of real estate, you should recognize a comparable home's lot size, square footage, architectural style, and amenities (such as upgraded heating and air conditioning, centralized lighting and electronic systems, and any renovations).

In addition, you must also know what the homes looked like before they were put on the market. A buyer may ask you why the home on 904 Sycamore sold for $1.2 million five years ago but is now selling for \$5.2 million. If you recall how the home appeared before the renovation, you can describe what improvements the owner made. You can discuss the new pool, the front yard that was extensively landscaped, and the kitchen that was remodeled. Now your client will understand why the house is selling for more.

There is yet another reason why the price for which comparable homes sold is important: Sometimes this figure is hard to access. This is especially true with luxury properties, where sales numbers are sometimes kept confidential. In the event that you don't know the sale price, consider asking your colleagues. With enough checking around, you can usually uncover the price.

Ponder the following fact: Most Californians move every seven years. Therefore, houses come on the market over and over again. The longer you are in your community, the more you'll know about changes within the neighborhood.

Often, photos on the MLS will show only the strong points of a listing. That's why I also encourage you to see the homes for yourself. Regardless of how detailed the information on a website is, you cannot substitute it for viewing the home, inside and out. Only when you actually walk through the property will you know which homes are on quiet streets versus busy ones, which homes are closer to traffic, and how good the floor plan really is.

COMMIT TO BEING AN EXPERT

Throughout my years in the industry, I've noticed a trend among brokers: Once a broker sells three houses, the fourth is easier. At this point, residents will take notice because the broker has created a track record of reliability. As you become more successful, your reputation will generate more business.

In addition, you will negotiate better deals if you've done your homework ahead of time and figured out the strengths of your listings compared to similar homes on the market.

Next, always fulfill your obligations. Remember that selling and doing a good job work together. If you market yourself as the real estate expert but fail to provide exclusive information, you won't succeed. On the other hand, if you market yourself as the expert and know your area better than anyone else, your business will increase.

In the beginning, you'll have many moments of frustration, and you may even doubt your skills. A way to counter these thoughts is to get busy. Visit homes, research your community, and create relationships with your colleagues. Your hard work will pay off. In the next chapter, we'll match your expert status with selecting the best homes for your buyers.

How to Find a Buyer's Dream Home, Even When it Wasn't What She Was Dreaming About

There's a lid for every pot. You may have to search all the way to the back of your cabinet to find it, but if you look hard enough, it'll be there.

—*Yetta Krul, my mother*

A couple of years after Saeed and I moved from Buffalo to Southern California, we decided to buy a home. At the time, I was pregnant with my daughter, Nicole. We were looking for a home that would accommodate this new member of our family.

I was clear about what I wanted and where I planned to live. I hoped for a home located on a desirable street, had a large kitchen, air conditioning, and absolutely no pool—I knew the dangers associated with pools and small children. I contacted a broker and expressed my wish list.

Richard, our broker, showed me several listings in Encino and Sherman Oaks. During our time together, he asked me questions and observed my reactions to what I saw. At the end of the day, he suggested that we look at one more listing. "It's not exactly what you said you're looking for, but you should see it anyway," I recall him telling me. He then explained that it was on the same block where he lived. I thought that an area good enough for my broker was good enough for my family.

Richard took me to the listing. They say that buyers make up their minds within 15 seconds after seeing a listing. I don't know how true this is, but once I stepped foot on the property, I immediately realized that the search was over. What surprised me was how little it resembled what I thought I wanted. In fact, in almost every way, it was *the opposite* of what I initially described. Looking back, I see what a skilled real estate agent he was.

I insisted on a one story home, this had two; I declared "absolutely no pool!" and this home had one; I wanted to live on the south side of the street, and this home was located on the north; I told him that I wanted air conditioning, and this home didn't have it; and I said that I needed a large kitchen while this home had a tiny one.

So what made me change my mind so swiftly? Richard paid close attention to my actions. As we walked through various listings he took note of my comments. He watched my body language: What features caught my attention? What did I clearly dislike? After figuring out my personality, he realized that I was a hopeless romantic: I love lush landscaping, expansive backyards with trees and flowers, and distinctive architecture.

What I saw in the Van Nuys home were cherry trees in full bloom, flowers, and a vast lawn, which were all the ideal setting for a pool. The architecture was not the ordinary suburban type, which often appears like a big machine stamped neighborhoods into existence. Instead, it was a two-story home that looked as if it were pulled out of a book of fairy tales. It had high ceilings, leaded glass windows, and a bishop's bench right by the front the door.

Upon seeing the house, I was willing to overlook all the details that I thought were *must haves*. All of sudden, the home's kitchen seemed cozy and quaint rather than small. Key elements that I thought would be deal-breakers for sure, such as air conditioning (if you've ever lived through a heat spell in Van Nuys, you know how stifling it can be), became less important. After seeing the home on Richard's block, my emotions tugged at me. I imagined myself living there and enjoying its amenities.

Shortly after, I phoned Saeed and asked him to take a look at the home. When he saw it, he too was willing to overlook what was missing in order to live somewhere that appealed to his aesthetic sensibilities. We drafted our offer right there, at the listing itself, and 30 days later, it was ours.

WHAT THEY *THINK* THEY WANT

In the example above, you saw how I thought that I knew what I wanted—until I saw something else. Your buyers are the same. I have countless stories of showing homes to my clients that resulted in the purchase of something totally different than what they thought they wanted.

"I want a Spanish-style home," a client will tell me. And just like Richard did with me, I'll listen, I'll observe, and I'll process this information. "I know this may not be what you were looking for, but I'd like to show it to you anyway," I'll tell her. The home will be a contemporary located in a neighborhood the buyer hadn't considered before. She sees the home; it appeals to her sense of style and taste, and she'll make an offer.

In your case, your job is to figure out your client's motivation. What is the driving force behind her decision? A buyer may think that she knows what she wants, and she may even insist on buying a specific type of home. Regardless of how certain your client may be, you'll be amused once you see how rapidly she can change her mind.

This, however, isn't always the case. If you know for certain that a client hates contemporaries, will never live in one, and will resent you for showing her one, don't do it. There's a big difference between taking clients to listings because you want to close the deal as swiftly as possible and making decisions based on the evaluations of what the client truly needs.

PEARLS OF WISDOM FOR THE BUYER'S AGENT

Your clients need your guidance. Based on their preferences, you must figure out what properties will best suit their needs. Here are three questions to answer when you're looking for listings for your client:

1. Why do they want to move?
2. What type of investment do they want to make?
3. What do they want to do with the home once they purchase it?

1. WHY DO THEY WANT TO MOVE?

When you're determining what type of property will appeal to your clients, figuring out their reason for moving is key. This critical piece of information will guide your search for listings.

There are several reasons for moving that you'll come across again and again. If your client has children, then schools are important. For instance, Beverly Hills has a great public education system. I know this because all of my children attended the schools there. In certain surrounding cities, however, the schools aren't as academically strong.

Letting your clients know about the quality of schools is important. To find out, experience is always best. But if you don't have children or ones that are enrolled in local schools, you can look at standardized test scores, which are usually published in the local newspaper and online.

In fact, standardized tests have become so widespread that a school's results seem just as important to buyers as their credit scores are to the bank. For additional information, you should also ask your colleagues and friends who have children in the neighborhood schools.

Another reason for moving has to do with age. Older people often want to downsize. I have a client whose children were grown and living away from the home. Therefore, Melissa and her husband were ready to move into a smaller house. They were both retired, and they planned to travel extensively. As a result, they wanted to get rid of the pool, the gardener, and the expense of maintaining a home with empty bedrooms.

I found them a condominium with a doorman. In their new home, they were freed from the responsibility of outdoor maintenance. With no headaches or worries about caring for their home, they could just lock up and leave for weeks or months at a time.

Additionally, you want to prioritize your buyer's needs. Some buyers are more concerned with a certain floor plan than a specific type of architecture. If they like the size of the kitchen and the master bedroom and closets, they'll buy it regardless of whether it's a California Ranch or a New England Colonial. Meanwhile, other clients seek to live in a specific neighborhood.

They're willing to overlook their preferences in architecture in order to have a desirable zip code. When you figure out your buyer's motivation for moving, you can focus your search.

2. WHAT TYPE OF INVESTMENT DO THEY WANT TO MAKE?

There are those who buy a home primarily as an investment that will earn them big returns. These people aren't concerned with how a home looks or what condition it's in. They're interested in finding *the deal*. Many of the homes these people seek to purchase won't appeal to a wide range of buyers. They may be hanging over a freeway, need extensive repairs, or have unappealing architecture.

Then there are those who are motivated to find their dream homes. Like every buyer, these people will consider price, but their primary reason for investment is to find something that suits their personality. They will often experience sticker shock, particularly in places like LA, because they'll realize how little they can actually buy for the amount that they can spend.

Your responsibility is to let them know that you will try to get them the best value possible and will negotiate aggressively on their behalf. In addition, it's important to inform them that they may need to make compromises. Regardless of how much they can spend, they might still have to make modifications to the home in order for it to meet their needs.

Here's a good rule of thumb: Houses depreciate, but land appreciates. In other words, God has created many things, but he won't create more land. If the home needs work but the location of the lot is ideal, then the property value has a greater chance of increasing.

If a home has good bones—an ideal lot, a solid structure and an efficient floor plan, even if it may need some work—it's a much better investment than a home that is in move-in condition but is located on a inferior lot.

3. WHAT DO THEY WANT TO DO WITH THE HOME ONCE THEY PURCHASE IT?

I once represented a friend who was a Hollywood producer. Liza wanted a house that was in move-in condition. This meant that she didn't want to invest in even a can of paint. I was researching homes for her when one day she called me. "Myra, I've found it. Will you come and tell me what you think?" she asked.

I met her at the listing. At the time, Liza was pregnant with her first child. She was in search of a home that was designed for a small family. Motherhood has taught me what type of floor plan would make Liza's life easier once her child was born. What I saw that afternoon wasn't it.

My primary concern was the floor plan: The maid's quarters weren't connected to the main house, which would result in the family's helper living outside the home. Furthermore, the master bedroom was upstairs while the other bedrooms were downstairs. This meant that once her child was old enough to have her own room, Liza would have to run up and down the stairs to attend to her.

I suggested that there were better choices for her, but she was insistent. Liza was attracted to the neighborhood and fell in love with the backyard, which seemed as large as a football field. She bought the home and shortly after gave birth to her daughter.

A year later, she called me. Liza wanted to purchase another property. The floor plan of her Beverly Hills home made motherhood difficult, and any changes would be too costly and time consuming. We found a home that better met her family's needs. The good news was that she earned $1 million from the sale of the house.

Her profit came largely as a result of three important factors: the home's location was extremely desirable; the lot was enormous; and she had a great sense of style, which was able to mask the unconventional floor plan. When she listed the home, it was full of artwork and beautiful furniture. When buyers walked in, they were oblivious to the floor plan because they were impressed by its overall presentation.

Once you've become an expert in your neighborhood, you are responsible to share your knowledge with your clients. Unfortunately, they may not always agree with you. In Liza's case, she bought the home even after I advised her against it. Despite my misgivings, she appreciated that I was upfront and honest. When Liza sought to buy another home, she realized that I would be the best person to represent her.

A significant part of your job as a broker is to be a teacher as well as a consultant. If you have exhaustively researched your neighborhood, you must be willing to express your suggestions to your clients. When they realize that you'll give an honest opinion no matter the outcome, they'll know that you have their best interest at heart.

Keep in mind that regardless of whether you agree with your client's decision or not, it's always important to remain positive. A good broker always focuses on bringing better choices into the search. Rather than saying, "This home is a terrible place for you to live," the skilled real estate agent will give the client more options to choose from. So remember not to waste time thinking about what is wrong or doesn't work. Instead, concentrate on the most favorable aspects of your current situation.

YOUR EXPERTISE WILL LEAD TO THE SALE

As I discussed in this chapter, your buyers may think that they want a certain type of property, but they may rapidly change their minds when you show them something better. This doesn't happen by accident. You'll only convince them if you have assessed their needs and have exhaustively researched your neighborhood. Here are three questions to ask:

1. Why do they want to move?
2. What type of investment do they want to make?
3. What do they want to do with the home once they purchase it?

Once you have answered these questions, it's time to match a home with the buyer. In addition, as Richard did with me when I was looking to buy a home in Van Nuys, you need to observe your client's reactions. What comments do they make? What does their body language say as they walk through a backyard? Their actions will guide you. As a result, you'll begin proposing options that they may not have considered.

In the next two chapters, we'll explore the selling end. I'll explain how to host high-impact listing appointments that will close the deal.

The Art of Telling Your Clients
That Their Perfect Home Ain't So Perfect

In Hollywood, the top actors and actresses know the value of leaving a lasting impression. They invest thousands, if not tens of thousands of dollars to work with the foremost physicians, make-up artists, and stylists. As a result, they're aware of how to look their best once the cameras are on.

As a top broker, you too need to be aware of what looks best. That's why identifying the strengths of your listings is critical. For example, some homes look better in the evening. It's important to schedule these showings at night. A home like this won't seem as appealing in the daytime because it may appear gloomy and unattractive compared to the light outside.

Likewise, if a home has an open floor plan with lots of windows and an expansive patio, it would be best to show this home during the daytime when the sun will fill the home with natural light.

As you walk through the listing, identify its strengths and its personality. Does it have French doors that open to a pool or a rose garden? Does it have romantic Old World charm, or is it an edgy contemporary? Just like you sell yourself based on your strengths—what separates you from your competitors—you want to draw attention to the home's strongest selling points.

If the finest features of the listing are easy to overlook, it's your responsibility to point these out as buyers walk around. For instance, let them know about the sophisticated security system that can be accessed throughout the home or the original stained glass windows that were recently restored.

On the other hand, a home's strengths may lie in what it *doesn't have*—it has strong potential, but it needs work. The listing may possess a fantastic floor plan, but it also has outdated cabinets and a central heater that needs replacement. As a result of the deferred maintenance, the buyer may be getting a great deal.

Knowing the home's strengths has an added benefit: It gives you insight into the history of the property. And when you know the home's past, you'll be able to share the information with your clients. After all, everyone loves a story. If a notable celebrity or political personality has lived there or if a famous architect has designed the residence, let buyers know about this.

Early in my career, I represented a buyer who bought a home that belonged to Theodore Roosevelt. It was located in the Flats of Beverly Hills. The property was an impressive brick structure that looked like something you'd see on the East Coast. It was impeccably crafted and built to standards that are rare today. Whenever I took clients to the property, their visits would be filled with questions about the home and its famous resident.

Later, I represented a seller whose home was the former residence of James Cagney. The famous actor lived in the Hollywood Hills property during prohibition—when the sale and consumption of alcohol was illegal. The house was complete with its own hidden bar.

The bottom line is, if there's a story to tell about the home, such as a vignette or an interesting fact, make sure you do your research. Then share your knowledge with your client.

WHAT TO AVOID WHEN SHOWING A HOME

Your goal is to make the home look the best it possibly can. But as any homeowner can attest, daily life, small children, pets, and years of wear and tear will inevitably affect a home's appeal. Following are examples of what you'll commonly see in homes.

CHILDREN AND PETS

These are often the center of a family. Unfortunately, their behavior can be unpredictable. Babies cry without notice, kids have tantrums, and pets can jump on visitors. So it's wise to have children and pets out of the house when you show it.

In addition, your clients' homes need to smell fresh and clean. Any animal lover who walks through the house will overlook the dog hair on the sofa or the litter box in the bedroom. But this can be a potential deal-killer if a person isn't used to or is allergic to pets.

If the owner has a cat, make sure that the litter box is outside when you're showing the listing. In the case of dogs, you don't want them around at all. You may interpret the Golden Retriever jumping on guests as a warm greeting; unfortunately, this behavior won't appeal to all buyers.

TELEVISION AND LOUD RADIO

Make sure these are turned off. They are distractions that take away from the home-buying process. Instead, I suggest that you play soft classical music at a comfortable level, one that will not compete with conversation.

CLUTTER CAN CREATE CONFUSION FOR YOUR BUYERS

When a home's storage spaces seem like they're ready to burst at the hinges from excess—too much furniture, piles of magazines, stacks of boxes, or children's toys scattered across the floor—you're putting the home at risk for not selling at the highest price possible. An overload of clutter isn't inviting to guests. In addition, a glut of goods makes an otherwise large home shrink in size and appear less clean.

Closets are another area that people overlook. Unfortunately, buyers like to look in them. They want to know that the rooms have ample storage space for their belongings. When closets are densely packed with clothing, they look smaller. Furthermore, stacked boxes placed high on shelves are potential hazards for your visitors; they can fall onto the heads of unsuspecting buyers.

In the kitchen, get rid of old pots and pans. Clear up the countertops and drawers as well. As I mentioned previously, buyers will look through cabinets and drawers. If a cabinet is piled with plates, Tupperware, and assorted mismatched mugs, get rid of the unwanted and unused items.

The refrigerator is another area that usually needs attention. Its doors are frequently a flat trophy case. A child's straight-A report card, Student-of-the-Month awards, and photos are often magnetically secured to the door's surface, while recipes, to-do lists, and invitations frequently coat its metal exterior. It's better to clear the doors of these items, leaving the appliance unadorned.

THE ART OF TELLING YOUR CLIENTS THAT THEIR PERFECT HOME AIN'T SO PERFECT...*IT'S ACTUALLY A MESS*

One person's junk is another's treasure. After reading so far, you may realize that a home you're listing is in need of help. You may look around and want to say to your client, "Put the toys away, toss the 1972 *National Geographics* in the recycling bin, and please, get rid of that awful purple paisley sofa!" But you don't want to offend her. Over the years, I've learned how to skillfully approach the matter of making suggestions to your sellers in a manner that gets the point across—in a kind way.

FIRST, ALWAYS FOCUS ON THE POSITIVE

Imagine that your client, Steve, is an avid hunter. His library showcases his greatest conquests—there are deer and elk heads on the wall and a bear hide on the floor. He's passionate and skilled at what he does. Unfortunately, these treasures could be deal-breakers.

A married couple tours Steve's home and falls in love with it. Until, that is, they enter the library. Their horrified expressions reveal their vegetarian lifestyle and PETA proclivities. The deal is off. To avoid this, I suggest that you compliment the seller on his pastime and the beautiful decorations in the room, but then let him know that for the sake of selling the home for the best price possible, it's in his best interest to put his trophies in storage.

I've read research that says people wear only 20 percent of the clothing they own while the other 80 percent simply hang in their closets collecting dust. In the event that there is clutter, for instance in the closets and dressers, I suggest that the owners sort through their clothing and decide if they can box what they don't wear. They can even send excess clothes to a charity and make a tax-deductible donation.

Remind your client that your goal is to sell the home for the highest price possible. Maintain the attitude that you're not only helping sell the property but preparing them to move out of it as well.

For instance, you can suggest that your clients begin packing things that they don't need right away, such as clothes that they aren't currently wearing, children's toys that are scattered on the floor, and artwork on the refrigerator. Let them know that this will make the rooms look as spacious as possible and, in the process, will also help get ready for their move.

THE KEY IS TO PLAN AHEAD

Earning your clients the best offer on their home requires preparation. As the seller's agent, your clients are counting on you to be their consultant. Thus, you're responsible for making suggestions that will lead to the sale. You also want to make this otherwise tense transaction as seamless and relaxing as possible.

When you initially walk through the home and assess its state, keep in mind that clutter could be a deal killer. Do your best to make the living spaces as open as possible. Be certain that kitchen cabinets, bedroom closets, and drawers leave enough open space for your buyers to be able to determine the size of the storage areas.

In the event that the home is consumed by clutter, suggest that your clients begin the packing process early. When approached tactfully, they will appreciate the suggestion. After all, this will also save them time during their move. It will make the home more attractive, bring a higher offer, and result in a quicker sale.

Be sure to avoid loud noises in the home, such as pets, small children, and music. If possible, have small children and animals elsewhere during a showing.

Next, invest time in researching the property. If buyers can easily overlook a home's strengths, then be sure to point them out. And if there's a story about the listing, be certain to tell it—people always enjoy hearing the history of a home. Has a famous writer, actor, or public figure lived in it? Is its architecture one-of-a-kind? Has a movie been filmed there? This step is critical to making the listing stand out from all the others a buyer is considering. The research will be well worth it when your clients get offers that they can't refuse.

In this chapter, I've shared the common mistakes that homeowners and their agents make when they are preparing a home for sale. In addition, I've explained the steps to communicate effectively with your clients. In the next chapter, I'll explain how to transform a home into one that will attract the widest range of buyers.

How to Stage a Home to Sell:
Appealing to All the Senses

Selling a home is like selling furniture. When you walk into a furniture store, flat boxes filled with dressers and tables that are ready for you to assemble wouldn't impress you.

That's why stores like Restoration Hardware, Ethan Allen, and IKEA stage their furniture in mock-up rooms. They know that you'll more likely buy a bed if it sits in a fully furnished space, complete with a rug, dresser, and artwork on the walls. Similarly, when buyers enter a home, they want to see how it functions.

THE IMPORTANCE OF CURB APPEAL

If you recall from a previous chapter, I described a home that I nicknamed Taco Bell because of its fast-food-inspired architecture. Whenever I would take clients to see it, I would preface our visit by describing its strengths. The lot was large and the views were impressive. In addition, it was in a good area surrounded by beautiful homes and excellent public schools.

Unfortunately, the house itself was a difficult sell. Over the years, the owners had made changes that took away from the home's original Spanish charm: A tile roof on the outside was met by a marble floor inside, and the finishes on the walls and the louvered window treatments were not consistent with the Spanish theme. The saying, "A little knowledge is worth no knowledge at all," appropriately summed up the appearance of the home.

To avoid this Taco Bell scenario, it's important to recognize the art of preparing a listing for sale. This involves not only setting up the home for public view but also matching buyers to specific properties. In the example of the "Run for the Border" listing, which was definitely not in turn-key condition, the buyer would most likely purchase the home because he valued the lot size and location, not the home itself.

In most cases, the changes that you suggest won't require that the buyer gut the present interior or tear it down and build another. Almost without exception, however, every home will need some modifications before the owner lists it for sale. As a real estate agent, it's your responsibility to guide your client. Your expert advice will prepare the home to sell at the highest price possible.

Over the years, I've learned how to do this. In this chapter, I'll describe the steps involved to make a home look its best.

THE DIFFERENCE BETWEEN
SHOWING A HOME AND SELLING IT

In the 60s, homeowners across the country were sanding over hardwood floors and covering them with shag carpet. Original wood countertops were replaced with the latest laboratory invention, Formica. During this time, the colors red and yellow were in demand, and refrigerators and appliances came in avocado green and harvest gold. Then in the 70s, the color pallet changed. Red and yellow became passé, and chocolate, rust, and beige were the *must have* colors.

A few years ago, the hottest kitchens had refrigerators, dishwashers, and warming drawers covered with panels identical to the kitchen cabinetry. Then stainless steel appliances became popular. Inevitably, these will be replaced with newer and more innovative designs.

Home interior styles change on a regular basis. That's why when you prepare a home for sale, keeping up with trends is important. The changes you suggest, however, don't have to be complicated. Simple steps like a new coat of paint and fresh towels and linens go a long way toward freshening up a home.

I once had a client who asked me to represent him because he was frustrated with his current agent. Scott's home had already been for sale nine months, and he felt that his broker wasn't effectively selling it. He severed ties with him and asked me to list it.

I met him at his home in the Hollywood Hills and immediately recognized the problem. Before putting the property on the market, Scott had moved out. Therefore, the house sat empty. Through my experience, I've learned that a vacant listing is a tougher sell.

As you prepare the listing for sale, you want to put yourself in your buyer's shoes. Assume that they seek answers to questions like, "Where would my couch go?" "Where will my children play?" and "How functional is the kitchen?"

In Scott's case, I encouraged him to stage it. This meant that he needed to fill the home with sofas, pillows, paintings, and additional furnishings. When I suggested that he hire a professional stager, he thought it was an unnecessary expense. I then told him what I tell all of my clients, "An empty house has no soul." I explained that if his goal was to sell the home quickly, the best way was to stage it.

He obliged. We hired a professional, and soon the house had been transformed from a barren space to a place that a person could imagine coming home to every day. The kitchen had pots and pans hanging on a rack and a bowl of fresh fruit on the countertop; the bedroom had comforters and a dresser; the living room was full of luxurious furniture that complimented the home's architecture, and artwork covered the walls.

You can imagine what a difference this made, and the results spoke for themselves. Although staging the home required a financial investment that Scott was reluctant to make, the property sold in three weeks.

You too must take on the buyer's perspective. When they approach a home, they are imagining calling it theirs. In addition, you want your listing to stand out from others that they will see.

To start, the seller could plant flowers along the driveway. The house should also have a new coat of paint, inside and out. If this isn't possible, the door should be newly painted and the doorknocker polished. And once a buyer enters, you want the interior to satisfy their senses: sight, smell, taste, touch, and sound. Appealing to their senses will create interest in the home that extends beyond words.

FIVE WAYS TO ATTRACT BUYERS

Regardless of how sophisticated or unrefined, rich or poor, all of us share something in common: awareness. Its basic nature comes before education and life experiences. Too many brokers forget this. As a result, they needlessly kill many deals. In this section, I'll describe how to use the five senses to get your listings sold.

SIGHT: VISUAL APPEAL INSPIRES CREATIVITY

When you prepare the home for sale, keep reminding yourself of the following saying: "You never get a second chance to make a first impression." Once you turn that knob and a buyer walks in, the house must look as inviting as possible. It must provide buyers with enough cues so that they can imagine calling the place home.

If it's daytime, your goal is to bring as much light into the home as possible, so draw back the drapes, turn the lights on, and open the windows and doors to the patio or yard. Next, have a fresh flower arrangement in prominent view. For instance, if there's a grand piano, place a vase filled with flowers on it. Here's an inexpensive flower tip: Buy orchids because they can last up to a month, look elegant, and add life to the home.

In the evening, you'll want to light candles. Candles not only provide light but add intimacy to your home as well. If the home has a fireplace, have it burning when your visitors arrive. If there are fireplaces throughout the home, I suggest that you turn them all on.

In the bedroom, I recommend a new comforter and pillowcases. After all, the bed is the centerpiece of this room, so you want to make it look its best. An attractive bed will make the entire space look clean, new, and inviting. Another tip: If you notice stained or dirty lampshades, replace them.

In the bathrooms, white, fluffy towels rolled up and placed by the sink give a luxurious image to the space. Fresh flowers and new soap sitting in a dish are simple yet important ways to improve the appearance of the area.

During the holiday season, you'll want to add decorations to the home. For instance, if it's Christmas, a decorated tree in the living room complete with white lights and ornaments will encourage the buyer to imagine that she may one day decorate the house during the holidays. Similarly, a wreath on the front door and poinsettias both inside and out are important additions.

SMELL: A MYSTERIOUS AND POWERFUL INFLUENCE

Humans have an incredible sense of smell. We can recognize thousands of different scents. The science of smell is so complicated that it isn't fully understood. Yet one thing is certain: A person's experience is greatly influenced by smell.

The scents we perceive have a strong impact on what we think. A certain smell can make us recall a memory from long ago. For example, the smell of hot bread can call to mind hours a mother spent baking in the kitchen. And a bad odor can make someone become physically ill without any other stimulus. That's why the smell of a home can have such a positive or negative effect on buyers.

I've filled the homes that I was selling with the aroma of foods like freshly baked cakes, cookies, muffins, and coffee. I've also complemented the freshly cut flowers throughout the home with fragranced candles lit on top of a coffee table or beside a bathroom sink.

In addition, the holidays are a great time to explore the scents that are common to those who celebrate them. For instance, Christmas cookies not only provide a snack for buyers but also fill the home with reminders of their own holiday traditions.

TASTE: OFFER REFRESHMENTS TO YOUR BUYERS

In a previous chapter, I explained how everyone appreciates a free gift. That's what inspired me to buy chocolate from my son's school fundraiser and give it to my clients.

So why not do the same for a showing as well? One of my clients provided fresh orange juice and lemonade to the buyers who walked through her home. It was during a hot summer, and the beverage was popular among visitors. This simple act left an impression on anyone who saw her home. Here's an even simpler idea: Stock the refrigerator with bottled water and provide it to your buyers. This is easy and effective, and I'm surprised how few agents do this.

Even better, baked goods draw on two senses: taste and smell. Filling an oven with cookies will infuse the house with scents that will soothe your buyers *and* give them something to snack on during their visit. Fresh fruit also hits two senses: taste and sight. A bowl full of oranges, pears, apples and bananas not only bring life to the room, but the decorations can be eaten as well.

TOUCH: FILL THE HOME WITH LUXURIOUS TEXTURES

What your clients see, they'll often want to touch. They may dry their hands with one of the towels that you rolled up by the bathroom sink. They may sit on a bed, feel the comforter beneath them, and look around the room. Or they may take a seat in the living room and consider what they like about the space.

Therefore, the linens that you use in the bedroom, the towels in the bathroom, and the surfaces throughout the home should all be clean. All of this preparation shows that the owner has paid close attention to detail, and this will leave an impression on your buyers.

If a buyer is clearly attracted to a listing, I encourage him to take a second look at the home. As he sits on the sofa, I ask what appeals to him. This is yet another reason why a furnished listing is more likely to sell sooner than an empty one.

SOUND: ENCOURAGES RELAXATION

Before a listing appointment, I walk through the home and draw the curtains open, light candles, open doors that overlook the backyard, and finally, I turn on the stereo. If the home has a central sound system, it's in your best interest to figure out how it works. Not only can you demonstrate the high-tech features of the television and home audio system, but you can also play music during the appointment. I suggest classical music at a low volume. Either bring a CD with you or tune the radio to a classical station.

A QUICK TIP ON SCHEDULING APPOINTMENTS

Once your home is ready for buyers to visit, it's time to schedule showings. Each appointment should be 20 to 30 minutes long. This will give your buyers enough time to look through the listing. At times your buyers may show up late; this is normal, and you should be prepared for this.

THE FIVE SENSES WILL MAKE YOUR LISTING SELL FASTER AND FOR THE BEST PRICE POSSIBLE

Appealing to the five senses requires preparation. But the process can be simple and inexpensive. In the end, whatever investment of time and money required will seem insignificant when the home stands out from the others that the buyer will consider.

Create a listing that is visually appealing outside with fresh landscaping, a newly painted door, and a shiny doorknocker. Inside, place fresh towels in the kitchen and bathroom and a new comforter and pillows in the bedrooms.

Fill the home with the smells of candles, fragrant flowers, or foods like coffee and baked goods. Then offer clients fresh apples from the display of fruit in the kitchen, a cup of coffee that is brewing on the counter, a bottle of water from the refrigerator, or a cookie that has just come out of the oven.

Finally, have textures in the home that appeal to a buyer's tactile sense—soft towels and fluffy comforters in the bedroom and clean upholstery in the living room will invite a buyer to take a seat and enjoy the home. Use the home stereo and play classical music at a level that can be heard softly, and turn off the TV.

In the last two chapters, we've covered the way to create high-impact listing appointments. Next, we'll explore how the Four D's of Real Estate will keep your list of clients growing.

From *Homemaker* to *Breadwinner*

The Four D's Of Real Estate:
Divorce, Debt, Death & Desire

In this world nothing is certain but death and taxes.
                                        —Benjamin Franklin

I'm sure that you've heard these words from the famous American. To these add two more—divorce and desire. Now you have the Four D's of real estate:

DIVORCE

DEBT

DEATH

DESIRE

If you're a good listener and have the patience of a saint, then the Four D's will keep your client list growing and the referrals coming in. To become an expert in the Four D's, you'll wear many hats: consultant, friend, mediator, and therapist.

For reasons that I still haven't figured out, divorce, debt, death, and desire come in waves. Sometimes it seems like all of my clients are selling as a result of a marriage break-up. Other times, family after family will ask me to sell a deceased parent's home. In this chapter, I'll explain the key qualities you'll need in order to succeed with the Four D's.

"D" NUMBER 1: DIVORCE

The statistics are no secret. In California, one out of every two marriages ends in divorce. With no change to this trend in sight, you'll always have plenty of homes to sell as a result of marriage break-ups. In order to manage a real estate deal that results from a divorce, here are four steps to follow.

STEP 1: THE FRIEND

Whether ugly or amicable, divorces are always difficult, so prepare to be a good listener. For instance, when a separation takes place, a household will be divided. Many times, the ex-husband and wife may not be speaking to each other.

I recall representing a long-time client. Max and I worked together for many years. In fact, I purchased his first home in Beverly Hills several years before he married. Now that he and his wife were splitting up, he asked me to sell their home.

Unfortunately, I was not a friend of his wife, Sally. Although we had no history of unfriendly behavior, Sally took the view that anyone who was a friend of Max *wasn't* a friend of hers. As a result, she was considering hiring her own broker to represent the sale of the same house.

Two brokers representing two people and one house is a complicated way to sell, and I let Max know this. He realized this himself but didn't know what to do. I offered to speak to Sally and clear up the matter. I recall my first phone conversation with his soon-to-be ex-wife. When I contacted her, she advised me to phone her lawyer if I had any questions.

"I'm sorry to bother you. I just wanted you to reconsider using another broker," I remember telling her.

"It figures; Max is always looking out for himself," she said.

"I know that this is tough time for both of you."

"It sure is. I just want this to be over," she said.

"This isn't easy for anyone. I deal with divorce all the time," I said.

"That doesn't surprise me." Her voice was cold and distant.

I explained how my experience had helped others through their messy divorces. I then advised her that working with two brokers would add unnecessary complication and stress to an already difficult situation.

Sally agreed to reconsider the matter; after our phone conversation, I believed that I had earned her trust. She phoned me a couple of days later and said that she was impressed with how I communicated with her and thanked me for being so professional.

STEP 2: THE MEDIATOR

Compared to what I had to deal with next, convincing Sally to work with me was the easy part. Yes, I was now the broker for both Sally and Max, but there were still two divorce attorneys representing husband and wife. If I made a decision about the sale, I had to contact Sally, Max, and their two lawyers. And both parties had different goals. First, neither would agree on a sale price. After arduous negotiation, the two attorneys and their clients settled on $7.5 million for the home.

Next, Sally wanted to sell the home as swiftly as possible, even if it meant that she would earn less. Max, on the other hand, sought the most money and was willing to wait until the right buyer came along. Under amicable circumstances, a couple like this would work out their differences. But because they weren't directly speaking with each other, it was my responsibility to relay information to everyone involved.

STEP 3: THE NEGOTIATOR

We based the $7.5 million selling price on comparables and on the fact that the roof needed work. Before we listed the home, I made some suggestions to improve its appearance. As a result, the owners planted flowers and shrubs in the front yard.

Inside, I advised them to make minor changes. For instance, I recommended that they purchase white sheets and linens for the bedrooms and hang fresh towels in the bathroom. At this point, the home was listed and ready for public view.

I hosted an open house the next week. A couple of days later, a buyer faxed us an offer. Once Max and Sally accepted, the buyers hired a building inspector. They looked through the results, and their broker contacted me.

The buyers expressed concerns about the roof, the plumbing, chimney, and the electrical system. As a result, they requested that we lower the price of the home by $200,000. I reminded the buyer that we had factored the deferred maintenance into the list price. Despite this, he insisted that we reduce the amount.

I contacted Sally and Max, and we decided to drop the home's price by $35,000. The buyers countered with a $150,000 price cut. After another round of negotiation, Max and Sally offered to lower the price by $75,000. The buyers requested $100,000. They added that if the sellers didn't accept this final offer, the deal was off.

Max, Sally, their attorneys, and I were in a bind. The owners feared that if we didn't honor their request, the buyers would walk away. We would then have to start the entire process all over.

In spite of their concerns, I suggested that the two take a hard line and hold to their final offer of $75,000. Sally wasn't convinced. In fact, she was willing to contribute $25,000 of her own money in order to meet the buyer's $100,000 demand. I remained resolute and told her to hold on to her money—the divorce had cost her enough, and she could find better ways to spend it. In the midst of this process, the buyer's agent phoned me.

"I can't believe you're being so tough," he said.

"I'm not being tough, I'm being realistic," I said.

"You know that there are other listings that my clients have been looking at. Like the one on Whittier—it's clearly in a better location."

"You're right. But if you think the roof's a problem on this house, you'd better take a look at the plumbing and foundation on that one," I answered.

"How about the house on Crescent? It's on a bigger lot," he said.

"But have you seen that floor plan? It's terrible," I said.

He went on to describe two more listings.

I finally told him, "Look. No listing gets by me. Everything you've seen, I've seen too." He paused and said that he would speak with his client.

As much as he tried, he couldn't intimidate me because I knew the inventory. I was aware of the value of the listings he had mentioned, their square footage, and their strengths and weaknesses.

The next day, I received a fax from the broker. His clients accepted our $75,000 offer. Upon hearing the news, Sally remarked that my advice must have resulted from a real estate sixth sense. My decision, however, had less to do with the supernatural and more to do with observing the deal from the buyer's perspective.

There were several factors that were in our favor. First, the buyers had locked themselves into a great loan that was looking even better because interest rates were climbing. Second, the buyers had spent thousands of dollars for the inspection and hours evaluating the results. If they walked away from the deal, they would have to start the entire process over again.

Finally, and probably most importantly, I knew the inventory. The other homes in the same price range would require considerable amounts of deferred maintenance. The buyers would find that any home they were looking for would need a similar investment to raise it to their standards. Once escrow closed, Sally and Max were relieved that one of the biggest hurdles of their divorce was over. Now, they could move forward.

STEP 4: THE PAYOFF

When I first contacted Sally, she didn't even want to speak with me; she mistrusted anyone associated with her husband. But after we had an open and heartfelt discussion, she realized that I was honest and professional.

Earning my client's trust is what I've built my reputation on—and so should you. Throughout your career, deals will come and go, but your reputation should always remain the same.

I contacted Sally a few days after escrow closed. When we spoke, she admitted that she was now one of my biggest fans.

She even offered to write a letter of recommendation. In it, she would share how I had effectively negotiated on her behalf during her divorce.

Successfully working with clients who are in the middle of a divorce is a test of your professional skills. You too may have to deal with a couple that isn't on speaking terms. As a result, you'll be responsible to relay messages to everyone involved.

Throughout the process, your clients will often express their frustrations, and you may act as their unofficial therapist. In addition, divorcing couples will sometimes ask you to meditate between one another and maybe even among their attorneys.

Under these circumstances, closing a deal that leaves everyone satisfied is tough work. It requires keeping your clients focused. This is a difficult task when people are upset with each other, blaming one another, or experiencing stress. But rather than spending time figuring out who is at fault, remind them that their goal is to sell the home, divide the household, and move on.

"D" NUMBER 2: DEBT

The real estate market is cyclical. When it's hot, buyers are willing to pay top dollar for listings, and the phone rings off the hook. And when the economy takes a dive, such as what happened during the dot.com bust of the late 90s, people will need to sell their homes due to debt.

In addition, you'll have clients who are in the red as a result of circumstances unrelated to widespread economic trends. Perhaps their finances are stretched because of one of the other D's, such as death or divorce.

During economically tough times, your clients will need an understanding ear. You're dealing with people who need to sell their homes and make a down-market move. At the moment, they may have the home of their dreams, complete with a pool, a large lot, and a view of the city. Now they're looking for a condo that is half the size of where they presently live. Under these situations, remember to treat your clients with compassion—it's difficult to downsize once you've lived large.

At all times, present your clients with a silver lining. Despite their frustration with having to buy a smaller home, there are positive aspects. For instance, there will be less to clean and less to manage. Remind them of the savings they'll experience when they don't have a gardening staff or rooms to fill with furniture. As a result, your clients will have more freedom. And if they have kids, they may be able to interact with each other more. Rather than having their children in another part of the home where they didn't always know what they were up to, parents will have them nearby.

I had a client who married a well-known movie producer. They lived in a large estate that matched the high-profile career of her husband. Their marriage took a turn for the worse. Kelly filed for divorce, and her life changed dramatically. She no longer could afford the extravagant lifestyle that came with her husband's job. When she met me in my office, I handed her a Kleenex to ease her emotional state.

"Kelly, I know it's a tough time. But there's a bright side," I told her.

"Like what? My marriage has fallen apart, and I can't stop crying," she said.

"Remember you complained about how much work it took to keep up the house?" I asked.

"Yeah. It was a pain dealing with staff—the pool man, the gardeners, housekeepers...*too much.*"

"I've found some great luxury townhouses. And think about it. You won't ever have to hire another gardener," I said.

"Myra, you always look at the glass half-full. Thanks. I've been feeling depressed and alone lately," she said.

I found Kelly a home that was significantly smaller than the one in which she lived. Initially, it was difficult for her to adjust, but once she did, she grew to enjoy her new place. Five years later, she contacted me again. This time, she had good news to share.

"Myra, I just got married," she told me.

"Congratulations! Who's the lucky man?" I asked.

"You'd think that I'd learned my lesson last time, but it's another Hollywood exec," she said.

We chatted about their relationship, and she then expressed gratitude for the support I provided her five years ago.

Kelly told me that she was prepared to buy another home. Her husband's business manager had lined up a broker already, but she insisted on calling me instead. As a result, I represented Kelly and her new husband in the purchase of a home that was even larger than the Holmby Hills estate in which she previously lived.

Five years earlier, if I had viewed Kelly's circumstances from strictly a sales and commission standpoint, there was little incentive for me to take her on as a client; I was busy with larger accounts and could have passed her contact information to a colleague. Instead, I placed more value on my relationship with Kelly than the commission. And when she remarried, she remembered how I had helped her—you never know how the kindness you extend to others will come through for you later. As they say, "What comes around goes around!"

"D" NUMBER 3: DEATH

Death is the most difficult of the four D's to handle. Not only is it an emotionally strenuous time, but in order for you to build your business with this D, you need to have strong connections within your community. For instance, Philip, a business manager, contacted me after his client died. I had helped him out over the years by providing his clients with evaluations of their homes.

Pro bono services like market analyses and home evaluations will benefit you later. In my case, I didn't know Philip's client, but my relationship with Philip was what counted.

In addition, when a parent dies, children are working with their parent's CPAs, lawyers, or financial advisors. When you work directly with these professionals, they will refer you, and you'll receive a phone call when the family is ready to sell.

Another approach is to scan the newspaper and read through the obituary section. Although I discourage you from becoming like the infamous ambulance-chasing attorneys, a kind note is a worthwhile expression of sympathy.

HOW TO PREPARE A HOME AFTER A DEATH

A home sold as a result of someone passing away often needs work. I had clients who had been married for 50 years. Ken died of cancer, and his wife Kathleen died weeks later. Over the last years they were alive, they had modified the home in order to accommodate their physical limitations. In the master bedroom there were hospital beds, and in the bathroom there were grab bars in the tub and special seats on the toilet. Throughout the home, the carpets were stained, and the interior was in need of new paint.

Before Ken and Kathleen passed, they referred their children to me. After their deaths, I met with their son and daughter. I let them know that for the home to look its best, they would need to spend about $20,000. They were reluctant to invest that much money. I added that preparing the home to sell at top market value would take additional time. They, however, were eager to sell the home as swiftly as possible. After I pointed out that the $20,000 investment would yield an additional $500,000 in the home's value, they rapidly changed their minds.

With the $20,000, I hired a professional decorator to stage the home. She started by removing the hospital beds, walkers, and handicap equipment that they had installed. After creating a clean palette with which to work, the transformation began.

First, the interior received a fresh coat of paint. Next, she hung artwork on the walls, placed furniture in every bedroom, and added simple, yet elegant accessories like pillows, throws, candles, and fresh flower arrangements throughout the home. The house sold swiftly, and the $20,000 investment seemed small in comparison to the profit the family made from the home.

In the end, I provided service beyond what they expected. Through this process, I also created new leads—when Ken and Kathleen's children want to sell or buy in Beverly Hills, Bel Air or beyond, they'll know who to call.

D NUMBER 4: DESIRE

As a new agent, desire is one of the best avenues for you to explore. That's because it's the easiest of the four D's to work with. And the good news is that desire is the most fun as well. After all, you're not dealing with divorce, debt, or death.

In fact, the circumstances are often very positive: Your clients have married and are searching for a new home; a couple's family is growing and they are looking for a larger house; a retired husband and wife seek to simplify their lives by moving into a smaller place; or a client is climbing the corporate ladder and is ready to upgrade. With desire, it's all about creating the circumstances where you're in the right place at the right time.

BE CREATIVE

There are simple ways to find your clients. Start with the newspaper. Here you'll find plenty of information. First, scan the business section. Inside, you'll discover who has been promoted within Dow Chemical, or if you're in Beverly Hills, who has become the hottest Hollywood producer. Once you know their names, send them letters of congratulations along with real estate information.

Next, check out the society section. Within these pages you'll see pictures from a recent wedding, or you'll read an article announcing a marriage. Send these couples a note wishing them well and provide them with a gift.

How do you decide what to give? If you recall from a previous chapter, I shared details about my modest beginnings. From my early days selling alarm systems and waterless cookware, I knew that everyone appreciated a free gift—regardless of whether they lived in Beverly Hills or The Bronx.

Providing something for free is a simple way to build a client base when you're starting out. If you're sending a letter to a couple congratulating them on their marriage, add a note pad with their married name on it. Or contact them and tell them that you would like to deliver a gift. Now you can set up an appointment and meet the wife, husband, or both. When you arrive, be certain to take the opportunity to share how you can find them their next home.

THE FOUR D'S OF REAL ESTATE WILL
DIRECT THE WAY YOU SELL

Life is full of ups and downs. Some years are full of good news: A couple gets married, a spouse becomes a partner in a prominent law firm, or a baby is born. Other years are painful: A loved one dies, a wife is laid off from her high-paying job, or a couple is splitting up. Throughout the good times and bad, your success depends on how professionally you address your clients' needs.

When you're working with clients who are in a difficult stage in their lives, do your best to be a good listener. Remind them that your goal is to make their lives easier by taking care of their real estate needs. And the best way to ensure that you're providing them service beyond their expectations is to be the expert.

Know your inventory. Regularly attend open houses and weekly caravans. Talk to your colleagues and share about your listings. How much are homes being sold for? What are the comparables for the homes that are for sale? Consider the impact you'll have when you reveal information about listings that they wouldn't have heard otherwise.

Send a congratulatory note to a newlywed couple. Tell them that you are an expert in representing first time buyers, and add a personalized notepad with their name on it. Or let the recently appointed CEO know that you specialize in the neighborhood close to her business and provide her with comparables. These are a few ideas; I'm certain that you can think of many more.

A good rule of thumb is that everyone wants to be connected with the latest information and trends. For example, every year, many business managers re-evaluate their clients' assets, one of the largest of which is their home. They do this for tax purposes and planning their clients' estate portfolios. Because you're considered an expert in real estate, they may ask you to provide them with comparable values of different homes in similar areas. As you do this on a regular basis, you firmly establish your relationship with the business manager because he trusts your expertise.

When the business manager's client is ready to sell his home, your name will be at the top of the list. The seller trusts his business manager, and the business manger is confident that you're the best broker to serve his client's needs. Providing evaluations may seem like it's not worth the effort. After all, it may take years before the client is ready to sell—if ever. But once he's ready, and you receive the call, you'll recognize the value of your effort.

Now that you know the Four D's of Real Estate, you're ready for the next step. In the following chapter, you'll learn what it takes to negotiate effectively on your client's behalf.

"What do you mean, the patio furniture isn't included?"
Keys to Successful Negotiation

Just a spoonful of sugar helps the medicine go down
—in a most delightful way!

—Mary Poppins

Back when I was starting out, I remember working with a broker whose communication style I will always remember. Whenever he talked to me, he used a very soft, hushed tone. Sometimes it sounded like a whisper. At first I was annoyed. "Why doesn't he just speak up?" I thought. But after getting to know him better, I got used to his style of talking.

Later, I realized that it was a smart way to work. When he whispered, I had to pay close attention. Otherwise, I would lose the message. Over time, I grew accustomed to his quiet tone, and in the process, I also found myself better remembering what he said because I had to concentrate on his every word.

Now, I'm not suggesting that you whisper to everyone with whom you speak; but it's important to pay close attention to your surroundings, whether it's the circumstances of the sale or what others are telling you.

Too often brokers are so preoccupied with closing the sale that they ignore the concerns from their clients and the possible problems that could affect the sale. In this chapter, I'll guide you through the ups and downs of the negotiation process.

THERE'S NO SECRET TO NEGOTIATION

With all the work involved in closing a sale, it often seems like you're pulling rabbit after rabbit out of a hat. But it's not about magic or summoning the supernatural.

Throughout the deal, both buyers and sellers want the same thing—the buyer wants to buy at the best price, and the seller wants to sell at the best price. So what separates you from your competitors? It's your ability to negotiate the best terms for your client, which requires you to rise above difficult situations.

A broker who gives up, believing that every deal is bound for disaster, will not succeed in this business. But brokers who have insight and experience will know how to overcome almost any obstacle that comes their way.

PROPER PRIOR PLANNING
PREVENTS POTENTIAL PROBLEMS

As the Boy Scouts say, "Be prepared." Planning ahead will give you the time necessary to handle the glitches that seem to come out of nowhere. Not only will this save you lots of time, but you'll also avoid problems that could possibly become deal-breakers.

For example, the results of the inspection may provide information that your client isn't happy to hear; the seller may not agree with the terms that your buyer has placed on the offer; and repairs may not be completed as your buyer expected.

Regardless of the challenges you'll face, as the consummate professional, it's your job to make sure that the deal flows as seamlessly and as stress-free as possible.

In addition, you must have the right elements to close the sale. As a good broker, you have to find property that meets your buyers' expectations, budgets, locations, and anything else they want and need.

Another important aspect of a successful sale is how you present your clients to sellers. If you're representing buyers, you should submit offers that are personal and leave an impression on the seller. This is because sellers often want to know details about the buyer. When they feel confident about selling their home to your clients, you've taken a major step toward having your offer accepted.

NEGOTIATING YOUR WAY OUT OF DIFFICULT SITUATIONS

In real estate, certain matters are predictable, like drafting a formal offer. Others aren't, like a client who expects more than you thought.

I represented a buyer who had found her dream home in Bel Air. Escrow was about to close, and the transaction had progressed smoothly. My client contacted me to express her excitement about the purchase. I congratulated her and complimented her on her good taste—the home was beautifully maintained and had an impressive view.

Julie especially loved the backyard. She described how her friends would enjoy sitting on the beautiful patio furniture that perfectly complemented the landscaped garden. Afterwards, I told her to contact me if she had any other questions.

I hung up the phone, sat up, and replayed her words in my mind. "PATIO FURNITURE?" I thought to myself. I felt my stomach sink beneath me. No one had mentioned patio furniture as part of the deal.

Julie never disclosed that she wanted to buy the furniture or include it in the offer. And now, as she shared this news with me for the first time, I realized she thought it was part of the home. "What would she say if I told her that the table and chairs weren't part of the purchase?" I thought. Before having this conversation with her, I decided to make a call that could solve the problem.

I contacted the listing agent and told him that my client was expecting the outdoor furniture to remain in the backyard. As I anticipated, he told me that it wasn't part of the sale— which was absolutely correct—and that the seller planned to take *all* of the furniture with him. Escrow was closing within days, and this could complicate the transaction.

You too might encounter such a scenario. And like Job from the Old Testament, your resolve is now being put to the test. In the art of negotiation, the key is to not get stuck in small details and to look at the whole picture, which means that you remain objective when you assess the needs of both buyer and seller.

In Julie's case, I knew that if the patio furniture was packed away in a moving truck, she would be furious. At the same time, the buyer had no intention of leaving it behind.

I was determined to continue the sale without the furniture becoming a possible deal-breaker. To accomplish this, I had to present my case to the seller's agent in a way that would satisfy both him and his client.

Initially, the seller's broker was obstinate. He explained what I already knew—the seller had no obligation to leave the furniture in the backyard. I then reminded the broker that thanks to the wonderful buyer, the deal closed quickly. She had submitted a solid, clean offer with only a few minor contingencies, and until now, this had been an easy transaction. I also shared that the backyard and its furniture were a major factor behind my client's decision to purchase the home.

The seller's agent agreed that the quickest solution to the problem was to leave the furniture behind. But he was apprehensive about speaking with his client. "What will I say to convince him?" he asked.

I advised him to begin his conversation by complimenting his client. I suggested that he say something like, "Because of your good taste and your investment of time and money preparing the home for sale, you're earning top dollar."

I added that the broker shouldn't focus on the patio furniture but instead emphasize the impressive backyard with its lush gardens and newly resurfaced pool. That way, the seller would see that the outdoor furniture was a tasteful complement to the overall appearance of the backyard.

This approach would help the seller understand an important point: It was a result of the seller's refined taste that the buyer assumed the furniture was part of the garden. I wrapped up our conversation by suggesting that the broker tell his client that although he was under no obligation to leave the furniture behind, it would be an unforgettable housewarming gift.

The broker appreciated my suggestions. After our conversation, he contacted his client. The next day, he shared that the seller agreed to give the furniture to the seller at no expense. Escrow closed, and my client moved into the home completely unaware of the work it took for me to keep the patio furniture in the backyard.

Whether it's outdoor furniture or an unfavorable remark on an inspection, the key to negotiation is the same—both buyers and sellers must feel satisfied. The two parties must believe that they are benefiting from the sale. Therefore, it's your job to bridge the gap between the buyer's and seller's objectives—which, in the case of the patio furniture, meant that I had to phone the seller's agent and persuade him to speak with his client.

As a result of the facts that I presented the broker, he believed that he had benefited from the buyer's offer enough to convince his client to leave the furniture behind. In the end, it's not *what* is said that's important but *how* one says it.

A good broker will know how to communicate news tactfully. He'll tell his client that he did an exquisite job landscaping the yard and had picked the finest furniture; he'll wrap it up with something like, "After all your work, it would be such a shame to take out the statue."

Unfortunately, too many brokers let their egos get in the way, and they hold to the last letter of the word. They are too busy trying to be the hero, and as a result, they stubbornly maintain their position regardless of how unreasonable it may be.

Success in real estate sales requires you to constantly adjust to change. Whether it's a change in the terms of the sale, a change in attitudes of buyers and sellers, or a change in the economy, your ability to adapt will take you far in this business. On the other hand, inflexibility doesn't help anyone and sours many a deal.

BAGELS AND BUILDING INSPECTIONS

Inspections are stressful events. When I'm meeting clients, they're typically anxious and eager to get inspections over with as soon as possible. Their hearts are set on buying the house, and their goal is for the inspector to give the home a clean bill of health. In fact, everyone involved—from the buyer and the seller to their real estate agents—wants the inspection to go smoothly. After all, the evaluation could make the difference between a dream home found and a search that has to start all over again.

Imagine that after two hours, the inspection is finally complete. Everyone is anxious to see the results. Unfortunately, it didn't go as smoothly as your client expected; he is frustrated and uncertain what to do. Next, combine these emotions with hunger: Your buyer is unhappy and also now hungry from the length of the inspection, and you are responsible to help him make one of the biggest investments of his life.

To help everyone through the lengthy inspection process, I'll bring along some bagels and cream cheese and pick up a few cappuccinos on the way. The inspector gladly accepts the snack because he's going to be working for many hours, and the buyers have something to eat while they wait for the reports.

Now when my clients hear the disturbing news, they'll be in a better state to assess the situation—a little nourishment has given them a chance to examine the report with more clarity. When you're hungry and tired, however, anything unexpected will seem more monumental than it may be.

ARE YOU REALLY LISTENING TO YOUR CLIENTS?

When you listen, you also trust your instincts. That feeling in your gut, that little voice in your head, or that intuitive sense is something that you should develop and follow. Learning to tap into it will be your most valuable resource.

I recall representing a client who wanted to purchase a home that was listed for $3.2 million. We submitted an offer for $3.15 million. The seller stuck to the $3.2 million, and as a result, my client was prepared to walk away from the deal. I knew that my client wanted the home, but he didn't want to pay any more for it.

I had two options. First, I could have directed my energy toward convincing my client to raise his offer to match the seller's price. If he agreed, this would have moved the negotiation process forward. Or, I could have focused on persuading the buyer to lower her asking price and accept my client's offer.

My intuition directed me toward the second choice. I knew that we had put together a solid offer, and rejecting it was a big risk for the seller. I phoned the seller's agent and our conversation went as follows:

"Frank, I know that your client wants the full $3.2," I said.

"It's a hot market and I think if we wait a little longer we can sell for *at least* $3.2, if not more," he said.

"But if I recall, the house was first listed for three months. After that, she got rid of her broker and hired you," I said.

"How did you know that?"

"I've been following it from the beginning. She listed it for three months, she hired you, and now *you've* had it for a month. You could wait for something better to come along. But are you ready to risk it? Especially when my client has given you a clean offer?"

Frank was receptive to what I shared and said that he would talk with his client. He called me later that day and said that he would accept my offer. What worked in this case was my direct and honest approach.

In addition, I knew the history of the sale—it had been on the market for three months already. After three months, the seller had fired her broker and hired Frank, so I knew that the owner was eager to sell. Furthermore, both Frank and I knew that once a month passes, a listing is not considered "hot property" anymore, and attracting buyers becomes a bigger challenge.

In fact, when a home remains unsold for an extended period of time, it often raises the eyebrow of potential buyers. They'll ask questions like, "This listing's been on the market for two months. Is it because there's something wrong with it?" For these reasons, accepting my offer benefited everyone: The seller received a clean deal after four months of waiting, and my client bought the home for a reasonable price.

HOW TO WORK WHEN IT'S HOT AND WHEN IT'S NOT

The real estate market has its ups and downs. When it's a seller's market, there are many buyers and not enough listings. Under these conditions, once a buyer wants a home, you'd better act fast.

Immediately after a listing appointment, you must be prepared to submit an offer. It may happen outside the home itself: You open your laptop and send the paperwork from your car. The offer is tens of thousands, if not hundreds of thousands, over the asking price. You know a good listing when you see one and convince your client to offer high in order to avoid competing for the listing. Meanwhile, the seller's broker sits back and waits while multiple offers pile on his desk.

Or sometimes the market is sluggish. You prepare a clean offer to a seller and your clients express doubt. You spend what seems like hours of your mobile phone's airtime convincing them that the real estate market is cyclical, that it goes up and down, and that it will all work out in the end.

In the following sections, I'll show you how to use your negotiation skills to close deals when the market is fully inflated and when the bubble bursts.

REPRESENTING BUYERS IN A SELLER'S MARKET

When the market is hot and homes are selling swiftly, you must work harder and smarter than your competitors—which means that finding the right home for your clients requires that you negotiate aggressively on their behalf. It's critical that your client submits a solid offer to the seller.

It's also a race to close the deal, with the winner being the broker who has the most information at hand. Whether it's the up-and-coming-home that isn't yet on the MLS, or the exclusive information another broker provides for you, your expert status is what will set you apart from your competitors.

For example, your connections will pay off when you're competing in multiple-offer situations. This is because your offer has a better chance of being accepted if the seller's broker already knows who you are. But before you contact your colleagues, first do your homework: Click through the MLS and attend Tuesday caravans.

Let's say you have a client who wants to buy a $2 million home. Ask your clients all of the following questions:

1. Do they have a lender? If so, are they pre-qualified?
2. Are they employed or do they have their own business? How long have they been working?
3. What are the reasons that they want to buy this particular home? (This will help when writing the personal letter that you'll see next.)

Once you have answered these questions, it's time to prepare the materials that you'll provide the seller once your client is ready to draft an offer. If your buyer is pre-qualified with a lender and her finances are in good order, a personal letter tells the seller that your client is serious about purchasing a home.

This letter is the schmaltz on the deal. If you aren't familiar with Yiddish, schmaltz is fat. It's that layer of cream cheese on your bagel or the rich dressing on your salad that makes it worth eating raw vegetables. A personal letter will bring warmth and individuality to the negotiation process.

When you break down a deal, it's really just a collection of forms and signatures. You want to add a personality to the offer so the seller can visualize the buyer and therefore stand out from all the others. The personal letter tells the seller to whom he is selling his home, for what reason, and what makes this buyer better than the others.

The following is an example of a personal letter:

Dear Mr. and Mrs. Myers,

My name is Matthew Carey, and I recently had the pleasure of visiting your home with my broker, Myra Nourmand. Over the course of several weeks, Myra has shown me many listings. After visiting yours, I'm now convinced that this is the place that I wish to call home.

At first, I wasn't certain where to move my family, so I decided to leave my choice to intuition: Once I saw it, I would know.

I was right. As uncertain as I initially may have been, your home is *exactly* what I was looking for. It stands out from the seemingly countless properties I've seen. It's obvious that you've invested a tremendous amount of time and energy into your home. From the elegant, yet understated charm of the interior to the expansive backyard, *I know that my children, my wife, and I will spend many happy years here*. If we would be lucky enough to purchase it and call it our own, we'll diligently maintain its character just as you have.

Three months ago, I sold my Hollywood Hills home so that my children could attend the high-quality schools in Beverly Hills. I have two daughters and a son, all of whom are school age. They are eager to begin their lives on the west side.

I am a television producer who works in Los Angeles. I have been in the entertainment industry for 15 years and realize that an opportunity has emerged for me to live closer to my work. As a result, I will be able to spend more quality time with my family.

I thank you for the care you have put into your home. I look forward to working together to make this a fulfilling experience for both of us.

Feel free to contact my broker, Myra Nourmand, if you have any questions.

Warmest Regards,
Matthew F. Carey

Imagine that you were a seller and received a letter of financial confidence from a lender, bank references, and a personal note like the one you just read. Now that you know the person on the other end of the deal, you'll pay more attention to his offer.

This letter is the last part of the contract. Before you provide one, however, make sure that you've done your homework: You know the neighborhoods where your client would like to live, what kind of homes are on which streets, where the schools are located, and the sales history of homes throughout the community, all of which indicate you're an expert in your area.

REAL ESTATE'S IN A SLUMP

As far as your clients are concerned, it's doom and gloom. They're reading the newspaper, clicking through CNN.com, and everything they see is the same: The real estate market is slowing, homes aren't selling, and the sky is falling. For example, after the Twin Towers collapsed on September 11, 2001, the real estate industry fell on hard times. People were afraid to buy. Meanwhile, brokers across the country feared that their real estate careers were over because the public's first priority was no longer buying and selling property.

When it's slow, when your voicemail box is empty, and when multiple offers are an exception, not the rule, it's time to approach the business differently.

In a sluggish market, your clients will require more hand-holding, and they'll need you to provide them with information that will make them feel secure about their decisions. They're worried about their investment. You'll hear questions like, "Isn't buying now a bad idea?" and, "In a few months, I'm afraid that the house will drop in price."

Here's where your expertise and salesmanship are put to the test. Yes, the home's value may drop. The price of properties, however, is cyclical. If owners remain in their homes for at least five years, history shows that real estate will bounce back.

Your expert status will guide your search. Because you know the market and the comparables, you know that you've found listings that are being sold at reasonable prices. In addition, you are certain that their investment is a based on *the guiding principal of real estate*—location, location, location.

Although the value of their property may decline, if its location is good, then it will ride out the dip and climb its way back up. When you're able to convince your clients that their property is being sold at a fair price and has the best location based on their budget, you've successfully proven your expert status.

Often you'll encounter that your client's fears are getting in the way of the deal. During these times, your focus needs to be directed toward lifestyle rather than the price of a home. Here's how to communicate with them effectively:

First, let them know that a home represents more than a price listed in an offer; their home will fulfill their physical and emotional needs as well. Ask them questions like, "Can you put a price on peace of mind?" and, "What is happiness, comfort, and relaxation worth?" Let them know that their quality of life increases when their children are attending good schools and they enjoy returning home every day.

Second, remind them that there are costs associated with waiting. If saving money means that for the next few months your clients will be living in cramped apartments with their belongings in storage, they need to consider the costs associated with rent, stress, and uncertainty.

WHEN TO WALK AWAY FROM A DEAL...*AND WHEN TO RUN*

Experience has taught me when to continue moving ahead and when to walk away from a deal. Figuring this out was like learning to drive. When you first get behind the wheel, you're uncertain about the distance you should leave between you and the car in front of you. You most likely have to go through a fender bender or two in order to learn what is safe and what isn't. Then, after years on the road, you drive skillfully and navigate around town without even thinking about it.

Real estate is the same. You win a few deals; you lose a couple; and you win some more. In the end, your losses have taught you a tremendous amount about how to be a successful broker and how to trust the inner voice that serves as your guide. Unfortunately, some brokers never learn to develop their real estate sixth sense; they're too preoccupied with closing the deal rather than paying attention to the details as the transaction unfolds.

When do you know when to walk away from a deal? Think of negotiation as a tree branch. The sale starts like a straight tree limb. You compromise. This may mean that you counter the buyer's offer by lowering your price closer to his. Now the branch is slightly bent. The buyer then receives the results of the inspection and insists that you drop the price even more. You look over the paperwork and feel like it's a reasonable request. The branch has a sharper bend to it now.

You're on the third round of negotiation, and the buyer now insists that all the furniture remain in the home, including the artwork that your client has carefully collected over the past 20 years. The branch cannot bear the stress anymore and snaps into two. You advise your client to refuse the buyer's request, and the deal is off.

Starting again is never something you and your client will look forward to, but sometimes you'll have to make tough decisions like these. Your client will seek your counsel and follow your suggestions. As stated previously, the more deals you do, the sooner you'll be able to assess a situation and make a decision that will benefit your client.

NEGOTIATION RULES OF THUMB

Keep the contract simple. When matters seem complicated, go back to the main points of your offer. The price, the terms, and the length of escrow should always be your guide throughout the negotiation process. Once you start negotiating about furniture, plants, and other personal possessions, the deal becomes complicated. The seller is often attached to his belongings, and giving them up may be a tough request to fulfill.

Remember, to become an expert negotiator, problem solver, and counselor, you must always bridge the gap between buyer and seller by providing solutions that benefit both parties.

With that said, if you're a buyer's broker and your client insists on having the custom-built sleigh bed in the guest room, it may be worth asking. You can let the seller know that it specifically matches the décor of the room, and the room wouldn't look the same without it. But you must use your judgment. If the seller won't budge, it will probably hurt the deal if you persist without coming up with an alternative that will satisfy both seller and buyer.

My point is this: It's never a black and white scenario in real estate. Sometimes you'll meet success despite nearly impossible circumstances, and sometimes a seemingly easy deal will suddenly require more work than you had planned. That is where your experience will be your best guide.

AFTER THREE COUNTER OFFERS, IT'S TIME TO MOVE ON

A home is often the largest investment that your clients will make in their lifetime. Thus, agreeing on the terms of the sale is often a complex process for the buyer, the seller, or both. This is normal. But more than three counteroffers is a sign that you should reconsider whether to continue the negotiation process.

Not only is the back and forth between the buyer and seller time consuming and stressful, but it will also become a confusing endeavor. Keeping track of the main points as well as what has been added, revised, and deleted is not worth the headache. As mentioned, the simpler the better.

THREE INGREDIENTS THAT WILL MAKE YOU AN EXPERT NEGOTIATOR

1. Gather all the information that will accurately represent your client.
2. Communicate skillfully.
3. Always adjust to change.

Before submitting any paperwork, gather information such as your client's employment, financial status, and prequalification letters from a lender. Once you have written an offer, draft a personal letter to the seller. This will leave a lasting impression on the homeowner. It also gives the seller peace of mind when he knows that his property will be passed on to a worthy buyer.

Your communication skills are critical in the negotiation process. Something that seems insurmountable, like bad inspection results, can swiftly be settled if you manage the situation with patience and a positive outlook. On the other hand, a minor glitch can swell into a deal-killer if you handle the situation poorly. The exhaustive research you've done about the listing and the impeccable offer you've assembled will allow you to negotiate powerfully on your client's behalf.

Lastly, you must always be prepared for change. From buyers, sellers, brokers, and lenders to inspectors and escrow companies, the real estate business is complicated. Even after 20 years in the industry, I still encounter new obstacles that I've never dealt with before.

In the end, all of your preparation will make the difference between an offer that's accepted and one that finds its home in a shredder.

The three components—collecting information, communicating effectively, and anticipating change—require skill and a positive attitude. When you believe strongly in the home that you're buying or selling, and the price is fair, then move ahead with confidence. Always show your enthusiasm; your positive outlook will become infectious. In the next chapter, I'll make the case for change—adjusting to the ups and downs of real estate is critical to your success.

Adjusting to Change:
Combining Today's Technology
With Old-Fashioned Common Sense

If you ever hear me speak, my roots come through the instant I open my mouth. My regional accent is something that I've grown to appreciate. This wasn't always the case. I recall having to stand up and read aloud in class. It's something that almost all of us in my generation who grew up in the United States did when we were in public school.

Kids definitely make an art form of pointing out the differences they see in others, especially their peers. When the teacher would say, "Myra, it's your turn to read," I could feel my heart pound through my chest. But this wasn't always the case. Reading aloud in Patterson, New Jersey, surrounded by kids who spoke like everyone else in Patterson, was easy. But when I was in Buffalo, speaking like I was from Patterson was considered strange and made me embarrassed to say anything. I swiftly adjusted and learned to take on the regionalism of wherever I lived. Today, my accent is a mix of different cities on the east and west coasts.

Through the experience, I learned to either fit in fast or slip through the social fabric that sometimes seemed more like a sieve than anything that could support me. Without knowing it, I was acquiring the skills to "make friends," as they call it in public school, or "allies," as they call it in war. I realized that if I didn't, I would soon become an easy target for teasing.

The social skills that I picked up while in public school and the sales techniques I learned from watching my dad made me recognize the importance of change. Success in real estate requires you to continually adjust to circumstances as they unfold before you.

BURSTING BUBBLES IN BEVERLY HILLS

In the early 90s, the Los Angeles real estate market lost its steam. In fact, conditions were so bad that it seemed like there wasn't even a drop of water to create vapor. Factors such as plummeting market conditions and the Northridge earthquake made many afraid to invest in real estate. This was a tough time for most agents because the prices of homes were unpredictable. In fact, you'd arrive at a listing only to realize that the debt on it was greater than its worth. Here is where an agent's sales skills were put to the test.

For instance, between the start and close of escrow, a home could lose its value. I recall having to allay the fears of my clients who were expressing buyer's remorse. I understood their anxiety. After all, within one month, the home they bought for $1 million was now worth $900,000. I was constantly reassuring clients that the real estate market went up and down over the course of time and that this was a home they would live in for several years.

At the time, the real estate industry was smaller and owned by a few recognizable people within Beverly Hills. These individuals built their reputations over many years of hard work. But soon, brokers couldn't pay the rent, the salaries of their staff, and marketing expenses.

As a result, the large real estate corporations, with their deep pockets, began buying out their smaller competitors. Meanwhile, many lesser-known agents left the business because they couldn't close deals under these tough conditions. Suddenly, businesses whose names were known across the United States began opening up offices throughout Beverly Hills, and the agents who previously had owned brokerages, often with their names on the doors, were now their employees.

THE ONE CONSTANT IN REAL ESTATE IS THAT IT'S CONSTANTLY CHANGING

Before e-mail, mobile phones, digital cameras, and laptops, agents did a lot more driving and running around than they do today. During the first few years of my career, my car's coin tray was always full quarters and dimes. In the event that I was running late, I'd pull my car over, drop some coins into a payphone, and contact my client.

Today, such a scenario seems almost implausible. Indeed, information is flowing faster than ever. On any day and at any hour, agents and their clients can log onto the MLS and see listings. Before computers, however, an agent used her office telephone, a newspaper, and her car in order to find out which homes were for sale.

Once the Internet appeared on the monitors of computers across the nation, many believed that the days of the real estate agent were numbered. After all, who needed an agent when a buyer could look at listings online and find information from a *Real Estate for Dummies* book?

In the past, buyers and sellers depended on their brokers to provide them with facts regarding their sales or purchases. But the Internet changed all of this. Now, real estate news moves rapidly from brokers to the clients, which means that if you don't stay abreast of the latest information, your client may know more than you. These changes have caused many brokers to retire their signs and throw away their business cards.

Experience has taught me that the widespread access the public has to real estate information has only made me a better broker. True, many buyers and sellers are logging on to the Internet to get answers to their real estate questions and to stay on top of the latest listings. But no website can replace the experience you have when you're an expert broker within your community. Therefore, I can confidently say that the relationship between a client and his real estate agent is as strong as ever.

STAYING ON TOP DESPITE FLUCTUATING MARKETS

My husband's philosophy has always been, "Money comes and money goes, but you can only build your reputation once." That has been the driving force behind Nourmand and Associates, which is one of the last privately owned brokerages in Beverly Hills.

What it takes to make it through the ups and downs of this business is—first and foremost—effort. Whether you've entered this profession when the sales potential was as endless as the view from a Hollywood Hills home or as slow as a 120-day escrow, one thing is certain: The market will change. Next, you must commit to being an expert.

A market at its peak will eventually fall into a slump, and a slow market will suddenly seem like it has endless possibility. Regardless of market conditions, your expert status is what will bring in business. It will make you a hot shot when there aren't enough listings to meet buyer demand. Your clients will know that you are the source of exclusive information about the local market because you know more about the homes within your community than anyone else.

It will also mean that you will work effectively when the market slows down. You'll suggest creative financing solutions and help sellers when they're frustrated with current real estate conditions.

THROUGH ANY MARKET, COMMIT TO EXCELLENCE

When a pilot takes off and launches into the sky, she knows her destination. She has planned ahead and has meticulously plotted her route. Throughout the trip, the plane will temporarily veer off course, but she anticipates this and continually makes slight adjustments until she reaches her target. You should do the same. You should have a plan that includes specific steps that will guide you to your goal.

If you've read this far, you probably plan to be in this business for a long time—you're not plunging into real estate only until you figure out what you *really want to do when you grow up*; instead, you're determined to become a successful broker.

Thriving in both good and bad markets can be a complicated process, but the fundamentals of success are simple: Focus your effort on the goal, which is to buy or sell a house, and adjust to whatever circumstances come your way.

We are approaching the end of our journey together. In the final chapter, you'll read about the initial experiences that provided a jumpstart to my real estate career and ones that made me want to abandon it once I began. Finally, I'll explain the importance of teamwork and how your support system will encourage you through both good times and bad.

You Can't Clap With One Hand:
Success Takes Teamwork

Success is contagious. So surround yourself with people who are successful and motivated. Remember, winners are made, not born.

Saeed, my husband, is a civil and structural engineer by training but an entrepreneur at heart. When we first moved to California, he quickly established himself as a successful professional. Once we moved from Van Nuys to Los Angeles, he took another big step: He earned his real estate broker's license, pulled together funding, and established Nourmand and Associates in 1977.

Those two years, 1976 and 1977, were significant for our family. In addition to the new company, our son Howard was born, and we bought our first home in Beverly Hills. It was a modest residence but a step up nonetheless. Five years later, in 1981, I gave birth to Michael, my third child. Two months after he was born, I carried him in a basket into our second Beverly Hills residence—it's the place we still call home today.

After founding Nourmand and Associates, Saeed's business flourished, and this provided the financial support that allowed me to be at home with our children. Allow me to clarify here. Between Nicole's tap, ballet, piano, acting, gymnastics, and auditions for TV and film; Howard's Little League, karate, soccer, swimming, orchestra lessons and saxophone classes; and Michael's basketball, swimming, baseball, and TV commercial workshops, I was with my children but *rarely at home.*

In fact, I had a T-shirt that read, "If a mother's place is in the home, why am I always in the car?" During this time, I created close friendships with parents whose children were equally as busy. These connections were critical to my real estate career later on. In the meantime, while I was home with my children, I maintained my own entrepreneurial yearnings by making custom-designed T-shirts and sweatshirts.

As my children napped, I pulled out the puffy paint, beads, stencils, and iron. Initially, I created clothing for my children's friends—shirts for birthdays and holidays where their names appeared along with a simple design.

Parents within Beverly Hills began seeing my shirts and wanting them for their children. Dance troupes took notice and ordered them for their performances. Ice skaters sought them for their competitions, and gymnastics teams requested team shirts. Over time, my designs became more elaborate and the projects more complex.

Meanwhile, my children were getting older and growing less dependent on me. During this time, Saeed suggested that I consider becoming a real estate broker. "Stop selling T-shirts and start selling homes," I recall him saying. I was reluctant to take his advice. I thought about how we would disagree on business matters, bring our office squabbles home with us, and soon enough take a number and line up at the Beverly Hills courthouse with our divorce papers.

His motives, however, were simple. First, he knew that I was a good salesperson. He also knew that I was well-connected to Beverly

Hills parents: I spent countless hours at PTA functions, on the sidelines supporting our kids at athletic competitions, and carpooling with other moms and dads.

Over the years, I had proven myself to my friends through my nurturing personality. For example, when it came to decorating advice, picking the best piano teacher for a friend's child, or finding the most qualified pediatrician, my friends looked to me for guidance, and real estate was a natural progression.

Often, while sitting in the bleachers cheering our kids on, my friends would share stories about their homes, what they were looking to buy next, and what made them unhappy about their current real estate agents. As I listened, I often referred them to Saeed or other sales associates within his office because I knew that they would take good care of them.

As I described earlier, there's a connection between selling and finding your niche. Whether it's the people you've grown up with or people with whom you share a common culture (like my father who set up shop in a Polish neighborhood), you work better with those to whom you can relate.

In 1988, I earned my real estate license. My business started in what are called the Flats of Beverly Hills. The Flats was the neighborhood that I knew best. It's where Saeed and I had raised our children.

I studied the inventory—in other words, the homes in my community. I researched the schools in the surrounding areas and found out which neighborhoods were suited best for large families, single people, and the elderly. Although this took time, it didn't feel like work—the true sign of finding a career that suits the person.

I've always loved to shop, and real estate became an extension of the pastime that I could spend hours doing. In high school, friends told me that one day I would be selling beautiful clothes in a Beverly Hills boutique. This was hard to believe at the time, considering the distance between Buffalo and Beverly Hills. But they were right...*well, almost.* Instead of selling beautiful clothes, I ended up selling beautiful homes in Beverly Hills.

MY FIRST DEAL

Kelly was a fellow mom in my child's school. Over the years, we had become good friends. While having lunch together, I told her about my new career venture. She was supportive of my professional endeavor and asked if I could help her find a home. Through that meeting, I not only sold her house in Holmby Hills, but I also represented her in the purchase of her new home for $2 million. After she bought her new house, I sold her former residence for $1.2 million, which means that I sold $3.2 million worth of property from the two homes—a significant amount of money in 1988.

My colleagues considered this first transaction beginner's luck. I had my own doubts as well. But any uncertainty I had of my ability to successfully represent buyers and sellers of real estate soon subsided. I worked around the clock meeting with clients, honing my sales skills, and researching the real estate market.

As a result, satisfied clients began referring me to professionals within the entertainment industry. My contacts within Hollywood quickly doubled and then tripled. In addition, I started working with entertainment attorneys who represented record labels and recording stars, as well as business managers of the celebrity elite.

At this point in my career, I am a thankful mother, wife, daughter, and real estate broker. As I reflect on my past, I am very grateful to my parents and in-laws. I recognize that there were many unhappy and often tragic events that had the potential of keeping both my parents and in-laws from reaching their goals.

For my mother and father, the traumatic memories of World War II and the death of their loved ones caused them to pull together the strongest resource they possessed—a belief in themselves.

In my father-in-law's case, he moved to the United States from Iran in order to keep the family united. He gave up being a successful pillar of society and having an extremely profitable business in his native land. Although his future in the United States was unknown, the rewards of maintaining family bonds far outweighed any misgivings he had.

From the very beginning, I was taught to persist, to work hard, and to value relationships. All of these qualities made me a successful salesperson.

IDENTIFYING THE STRENGTHS OF THOSE AROUND YOU

Saeed and I have different personalities, which is obvious by our tastes in books and television programs. If the TV remote control was in his hands, he would flip to the Discovery Channel, the History Channel, and science programs on PBS. I, on the other hand, would tune to comedies, dramas, and romance.

Saeed has an analytical mind. In fact, in his spare time he is an inventor, holding patents in his name. When we watch "who dunnit" films, within 10 minutes, he's figured out who committed the crime and how it happened. Meanwhile, I'm focusing on character development and the actors' performances.

We came from different countries, spoke different languages at home, and had noticeably different childhood experiences. But what we shared in common was far more important than any dissimilarity. We were both raised in loving households with mothers and fathers who instilled values that transcended the gaps between his culture and mine. This appreciation and commitment to family gave us an immediate connection when we first met.

Saeed recognized the potential in me, and he was precisely the person I needed to overcome my fears and to push ahead. During those early days, every experience was a valuable lesson. I recall finding a listing for one of my clients, an executive in the entertainment industry. Andrew saw the Holmby Hills home and was motivated to buy. We made an appointment to meet.

Andrew and his wife arrived at my office. He had an imposing figure and smoked a cigar, which left a trail of second-hand smoke wherever he walked. I invited the couple into my office and requested verification regarding their down payment.

"I'll just need something in writing," I recall telling the couple.

Both were silent. But Andrew's response was a stare that signaled that I had said something terribly offensive. He glared at the offer that was on my desk.

"What do you mean, 'you'll need something in writing?'" he asked.

"You know, routine paperwork. It's all part of the offer we'll give to the seller," I said.

"Are you saying that you don't think I can pay? Let me tell you something. I've got enough money to buy that place in cash.

And I don't need a letter to prove it," he said.

He then extended his arm toward my desk, grabbed the contract, and crumpled it in his hands. He spat on it and used the tip of his shoe to grind it into the carpet.

"That's what I think of your offer." He let out a huff, rose from his chair, and left my office.

His wife looked at me with embarrassment yet said nothing. Her reaction told me that this wasn't the first time she'd stood by him during one of his tantrums. She silently followed after him as he left behind the invisible stench of cigar smoke and a crumpled, saliva-coated piece of paper.

Once he left, I phoned my husband to tell him what had just happened. I wanted him to know how disrespectful Andrew had been and how I had no desire to work with someone who had such a bad temper.

"Myra, I know you're upset," he said.

"He was so rude! I was even afraid for my own safety," I said.

"I think that you should send him flowers," he said.

"Flowers? For what...his smelly cigar?"

"Send him flowers then tell him you're sorry that he was inconvenienced," he said.

His suggestion was absurd. Why would I want to show any courtesy to the man who had insulted me in my own office?

Saeed's wisdom, however, had helped me in the past, so despite my reservations, I ordered flowers and had them delivered to Andrew. He phoned me the next day to thank me for the beautiful arrangement. In his own way, without saying the words "I'm sorry," Andrew was expressing regret for what he had done.

My husband is a logical thinker. In Andrew's case, he suggested that I do the unthinkable. After hearing his advice, I thought to myself, "Wouldn't sending flowers be an admission of guilt?" and "I owe this rude man nothing!"

In the end, extending an olive branch toward my client was prudent advice.

From this example, you can see that Saeed and I work as a team. So much of being married is about listening to one another. Although we have different personalities, we focus on our strengths, and this has made our relationship stronger.

YOUR TEAM WILL HELP
YOU REACH YOUR GOALS FASTER

Education was a top priority in our house, so schoolwork was always completed on time. Well, almost always. During busy afternoons, the kids did their homework in the backseat as I drove them to their next practices. Sometimes, making sure that they completed their work required even more effort.

I recall the volcano projects that were due the next morning: My son was passed out on the couch from a long day of activity. Meanwhile, Saeed worked until 4:00 a.m. ensuring that the baking soda and vinegar successfully erupted out of the mouth of a hand-painted mountain.

Now that I was a broker, I still had the same commitment to my kids, but I was also attending meetings, open houses, and building a client base. During these busy times, my mother-in-law, Lili, came to the rescue. Without her, I would not be the businessperson I am today.

For instance, if a meeting ran long and I couldn't pick up Howard or Michael from practice, she would make sure that they arrived home safely. When I wasn't able to take Nicole to a rehearsal, Lili or my sister-in-law, Fay, would arrange the carpooling. Their support meant that I didn't have to give up being a parent in order to keep my career going.

That's why I can never attribute my accomplishments solely to my own effort. Thanks to the support of those closest to me, I was able to maintain focus—even after a client would yell at me, a deal had gone badly, or when I was exhausted and questioned whether I should continue in this profession.

In your case, you may not have a built-in support system, but that doesn't mean that you can't create one. For example, if you have children, you can organize study and play dates with other parents. This will open up time for you to invest in your business.

Also, consider creating a carpool schedule with other parents so you all share the responsibility of driving kids to school and extracurricular activities. Make arrangements with friends and colleagues ahead of time so someone can supervise your children in the event that you have to show a home last-minute or obtain a signature on an offer.

There are other significant ways to build your business if you don't have children. You can generate business contacts through volunteer work. For instance, you may be active in a charity, a philanthropic group, or in sports such as baseball and football. Regardless of what your interest is, your activity will not only support your community, but it will also be a resource for clients and business.

TEAMWORK WILL CARRY
YOU THROUGH DIFFICULT TIMES

As I shared earlier, at first I had many doubts about my career choice. Even when I earned my first commission check, the words, "You're only as successful as your last sale" swirled in my mind. After a few deals, however, I knew that I had found my career calling.

This isn't to say that it was easy. I went through countless boxes of Kleenex as a result of frustration, self-doubt, and being treated badly by others. The first few months were a test of my personal resolve.

Every day, I'd arrive at the office after dropping my kids off at school. I'd sit at my desk and pick up the telephone. These two tools—my desk and phone—were my entrance into the real estate business. I would flip through my list of prospective clients: parents from my children's school, friends, and family members.

My enthusiasm was tough to maintain. A strong lead would give me hope while a rude agent would make me question why I was doing this in the first place. I remember presenting an offer to a broker in his office; my client wanted to buy the house very much, and I was working aggressively on his behalf.

When I showed up at the agent's office, there was another broker putting in an offer for the same house. I then realized that the home was in multiples and competition would be fierce. The other agent clearly thought the same thing. As she handed her paperwork to the broker, she turned around and stared at me.

"Myra Nourmand...what are you doing here?" she asked. Without letting me answer she said, "Let me guess. You're putting in an offer too. Just what I need today...another listing gone into multiples."

"Yeah, but I see that you beat me to it," I said in an attempt to lighten things up.

She plopped the paperwork on the broker's desk and faced

me. Then she reached down and took her shoe off.

"And I thought I'd be the last one here today. Thanks a lot," she said pointing her pump at me. She hurled her shoe at the floor and limped out of the office.

If that were to happen today, I would reflect on the event and realize how silly her behavior was—experience has taught me to let reactions like hers bounce right off me. But back then, what took place meant that I would peel open another box of Kleenex.

During these times, Saeed was there to listen. But he never allowed me to dwell on my problems for long. When I would complain about colleagues—brokers who cut corners and agents that were unprofessional—he reminded me that I worked different-ly, and this is what would make me shine. His attitude heavily influenced the way I work today.

As my business has grown, I've become more assertive and willing to express my opinions more freely. I realize that my actions and beliefs impact the lives of others. From the begin-ning, Saeed knew that I had sales experience and that I worked hard. What he didn't realize was how motivated I was to rise to the top of my field. In fact, we've both been equally amazed with my success.

YOU'VE BEEN MULTITASKING ALL YOUR LIFE; NOW GET PAID TO DO IT

Through the experiences that I've shared in this book, you can see how the lessons you've learned throughout your life will help you in your career. The skills you've used to organize a child's soccer team, charity event, or party are the same as those you'll employ to juggle appointments and schedule showings.

REAL ESTATE IS A MOST PERSONAL ENDEAVOR

Selling and buying homes is one of the most intimate business transactions you can make. As a broker, you play a central role in this private endeavor. You're responsible to find a place for your clients to live, and in many instances, you're helping them make landscaping and interior decorating decisions.

When you're showing a house to a buyer, you're entering bedrooms, pulling out closet drawers, and opening shower doors. Sometimes it seems like the only thing you're not doing is picking out a client's suit and putting it in his closet.

TREAT YOUR CLIENTS AS YOUR FRIENDS

Many of my clients have become my close friends as well. The opposite is true also—the friends that I made while raising my kids became my clients. In fact, during the holidays, I spend hours in the kitchen cooking and baking for our parties. Our home is filled with guests whom we've represented in home sales and purchases; they've become extended members of our family.

I once represented a movie producer in the purchase of his Bel Air estate. He sold his Beverly Hills residence, and escrow had just ended on his family's new home.

It was spring, and the notorious Santa Ana winds of Southern California created brush fires in Los Angeles. With the streets around his neighborhood closed, his family's belongings were trapped in moving vans that were prohibited from entering Bel Air.

In the meantime, the family of four stayed in a hotel. It was the holiday season, and they didn't have a place where they could celebrate. That night, my husband and I invited them to our home where they enjoyed a home-cooked meal with our family.

MAKE THIS JOB THE BEST YOU'VE EVER HAD

At some point in your life, you've probably been given the advice to find a job that you love doing. After all, you spend most of your life working, so it makes sense to earn money *and* enjoy what you do every day.

Flexibility is one of the best aspects of this profession. Real estate is not a 9–5 job where you're stuck in a cubicle fulfilling the demands of your boss. Instead, it's accommodating, always changing, and rewarding.

If you have a family, you can work around a schedule that will allow you to meet your responsibilities as caregiver. And there is no room for boredom in this profession because you're dealing with clients who are always challenging you with new experiences.

In fact, you'll continually meet people from all walks of life— individuals like actors, CFOs, entrepreneurs, politicians, and celebrities. This opportunity to work with such a wide range of successful people is common for top brokers. In real estate, you're selling dreams and making them a reality, and you'll continually encounter interesting people.

THIS IS SERIOUSLY FUN BUSINESS

Throughout the years, I've developed many connections within my community. Often, when I'm attending a party, someone will approach me and say something like, "Myra, I love my home. Thanks for guiding me when I was so worried. Your encouragement and patience got me through a tough time." Comments like these make me proud of my work and remind me how important my job is.

After all, a home is one of the biggest financial investments that your clients will make. It's also the place where they'll raise their children, entertain friends and family, and create countless memories. In the end, it's because of you that your clients have found a home that they look forward to coming home to every day.

WHAT GOES AROUND COMES AROUND

Allow me to briefly indulge in the metaphysics of real estate. If you haven't already, you'll rapidly realize that the real estate community is small—and what goes around comes around. People talk, reputations are made, and referrals sometimes seem to come out of thin air. From the children of clients you've had in the past to business managers and attorneys you've worked with before, you never know how the relationship that you value today will benefit your business months or years later.

As a broker, you tremendously influence the direction that your clients' lives will take. A home that meets their needs will provide them years of pleasure, while a half-hearted sale focused only on the bottom line could result in an immense amount of stress and unhappiness for your client. That's why this business is more than a way to earn quick cash. Once you view this job as a moneymaking endeavor only, you should look for another career.

I once had a prospect contact me for selling advice. I visited his home, and after hearing his reasons for selling, I recommended that he keep it. "I can't believe that you'd suggest such a thing," I recall him saying.

"I've got to be honest with you—I've listened, and I see that it's best for you not to sell," I said.

"Myra, thanks for not jumping on the chance to earn a commission. And I know that you're not making a dollar giving me your advice," he said.

Months later he contacted me again. He shared his reasons for selling, and this time I agreed with him. I asked him why he decided to work with me.

"All the other brokers I spoke to only wanted the deal. But you were different. You were looking out for me and didn't care about the commission. That's impressive," he said.

You've got to think beyond the monetary rewards and place all of your energy into providing service that benefits your clients. Working this way will lead to long-term success.

DO UNTO OTHERS AS YOU
WOULD HAVE THEM DO UNTO YOU

The following is how the Golden Rule plays out in real estate: Be respectful of your client's time; be caring and concerned about your client's interests; be an expert; and do your homework. From the Bronx to Bel Air, this is the formula for success. Working this way will lead to a career filled with satisfaction, and new friendships that will help you become an influential member of your community.

By following my methods and principals that I've described throughout this book, you'll reach your financial goals, know that you're the best that you can be, and play a central role in one of the most significant decisions that your clients will ever make.

I'll conclude by sharing the secret to what will make this job the best you've ever had: Make work fun. This is a tough business, and success only comes to those who work the hardest. Therefore, humor and laughter are critical ingredients that will make the process pleasurable. You're improving the lives of those around you; take pride in that and enjoy yourself.

I hope you find your career in real estate more fulfilling and lucrative than any you've ever imagined, and I wish you years of success. Now it's time to create the experiences that will fill the pages of *your* book. Remember, your success is in your hands, so show, sell, and close those deals!

Index

A

Aesthetic sensibilities, 63–65
Age, as reason for moving, 67
Agent. *See* Buyer's agent; Real estate agent; Seller's agent
Appointments. *See also* Showings being on time to, 45
Appreciation, of land, 68–69
Attitude, positive, 77–79, 98–99

B

Bathrooms, preparation for showings, 85–86
Bedrooms, preparation for showings, 85
Board of Realtors, regulations of, 45
Building inspections, 111
Buyers, attracting, 84–88
Buyer's agent
in negotiation, 107
questions for, 66–71
in seller's market, 114–117
Buyer's remorse, 124

C

Candles, at showings, 85
Caravans, weekly, 58, 60
Change, adjusting to, 110, 123–128
Children
of clients, 32–33
and showings, 75
Client(s)
building base of, 27–28, 29, 32, 38, 100, 102–103, 130, 131, 141–142
children of, 32–33
communication with, 77–78
dream homes of, 63–71
as friends, 140–141
investment desires of, 68–69

knowledge of, 63–71
listening to, 34, 112–113
making assumptions about, 43–45
prioritization of needs of, 67–68
questions for, 66–71
reasons for moving, 66–68
respect of, 37
similarities with, 31
traveling to showings with, 33
Closets, preparation for showings, 76, 78
Clutter, eliminating, 76–77, 78–79
Colleagues, relationships with, 58
Communication
with clients, 77–78
style of, 105
Community
driving around, 55–56, 60
knowledge of, 36–37, 42–43, 49–50, 53–54, 59–60, 70, 95–96
Comparables, 60–61, 104
Competition, 57
Confidence, 46
Contact list. *See* Client(s)
Contracts, simple, 120
Counter-offers, 121
Curb appeal, 81–82
Current events, keeping up with, 34

D

Death, 91, 100–101
Debt, 91, 97–100
Desire, 91, 102–103
Divorce, 91, 92–97
Downsizing, 67, 98
Driving
around community, 55–56, 60
to showings with clients, 33
D's of Real Estate, Four, 91–104

Death, 100–101
Debt, 97–100
Desire, 102–103
Divorce, 92–97

E
Effort, 39, 40–42, 47
Emotions, in real estate
  purchases, 63–65
Enthusiasm, 46–47, 48
  definition of, 39
  and expertise, 47
E's of Success, Four, 39–48
  Effort, 40–42, 47
  Enthusiasm, 46–47, 48
  Ethics, 43–46, 48
  Expertise, 42–43, 47–48, 49–62
Ethics, 39, 43–46, 48
Excellence, commitment to, 127–128
Expertise, 42–43, 47–48, 49–62
  commitment to, 61–62
  definition of, 39
  and enthusiasm, 47
  homework/research and, 54–55
  lessons concerning, 56–57
  in seller's market, 114
  specialized knowledge and, 49–53
  technology and, 53–54, 55–57,
  125–126

F
Fireplaces, 85
Flexibility, 40, 110, 123–128, 141
Flowers, at showings, 85
Fluctuations, in real estate market,
  113–118, 124–125, 126–127
Follow-up, 45
Four D's of Real Estate, 91–104
  Death, 100–101
  Debt, 97–100
  Desire, 102–103
  Divorce, 92–97
Four E's of Success, 39–48
  Effort, 40–42, 47
  Enthusiasm, 46–47, 48
  Ethics, 43–46, 48
  Expertise, 42–43, 47–48, 49–62

Friend(s)
  clients as, 140–141
  real estate agents as, 92–93,
  140–141
Fun, at work, 34–36, 141–142, 144

G
Gift giving, 29–32, 102–103
Give before getting, 99–100, 143–144
Golden Rule, 143–144

H
History, of property, 74–75
Holiday seasons, showings
  during, 86
Hollow clay tile structures, 51–53
Hollywood Athletic Club, 52
Homes, nicknames for, 35–36
Honesty, 70–71

I
Incentives, 29–32, 102–103
Inspections, 111
Insurance risks, 41
Interior styles, changes over time, 83
Internet, 53–54, 125–126. *See also*
  Technology
Inventory, knowledge of, 36–37,
  42–43, 49–50, 59–60, 70, 95–96
Investment, type of, 68–69

K
Kitchen, preparation for
  showings, 76–77
Knowledge
  of clients, 63–71
  of community/inventory, 36–37,
  42–43, 49–50, 53–54, 59–60, 70,
  95–96
  specialized, 49–53

L
Land, appreciation of, 68–69
List price, justification of, 60–61
Listening, to clients, 112–113
Listings
  furnished, 88

history of, 74–75
knowledge of, 36–37, 42–43, 49–50, 53–54, 59–60, 70, 95–96, 112–113
personal familiarity with, 61
previewing, 58
staging of, 81–89, 101
strengths of, 73–74
weekly caravans of, 58, 60
Location
  importance of, 68–69
  and insurance risks, 41
  in market slump, 118
Los Angeles, 1990's real estate market of, 124–125

M
Mediator, real estate agent as, 93–94
Motherhood, benefits to professional life, 28–29
Moving, reasons for, 66–68
Multitasking, 139
Music, at showings, 76

N
Needs, prioritization of, 67–68
Negotiation, 105–122
  components of, 121–122
  counter-offers in, 121
  flexibility in, 110
  obstacles in, dealing with, 40, 106, 107–110
  preparation for, 106–107
  rules of thumb for, 120–121
  walking away from, 119–120
Negotiator, real estate agent as, 94–96
Networking, 27–28, 29, 32, 38, 100, 130, 131, 141–142
Nicknames, for homes, 35–36
Nourmand, Myra, biography of, 11–21
Nourmand and Associates, founding of, 129

O
Obstacles, in negotiation, dealing with, 40, 106, 107–110
Open houses, 60. *See also* Showings

P
Personal reference letter, in seller's market, 115–117
Pets, and showings, 75
Positive attitude, 77–79, 98–99
Preview, of listings, 58
Prioritization, of client needs, 67–68
Pro bono services, 100
Property value, 68–69

R
Radio, at showings, 76
Real estate
  Four D's of, 91–104
  getting started in, 27–28
  personal stakes in, 140
Real estate agent
  decision to become, 27–28
  as friend, 92–93, 140–141
  as mediator, 93–94
  as negotiator, 94–96
  as teacher, 36–37
Real estate market
  fluctuations in, 113–118, 124–125, 126–127
  in 1990's Los Angeles, 124–125
  risky locations, 41
  seller's market, 113–117
  slump, 40–42, 113–114, 117–118
Real estate purchase, purpose of, 69–71
Real estate sale, example of, 132–133
Reference letter, personal, in seller's market, 115–117
Refreshments
  at building inspections, 111
  at showings, 87
Refrigerator, preparation for showings, 76–77
Regulations, of Board of Realtors, 45
Renovations, 60–61

Reputation, 45, 47, 142–143
Respect, 37
S
Sale, example of, 132–133
Salesmanship, 30–31
Scheduling, of showings, 88
Schools, knowledge of local, 66–67
Seller's agent
  in negotiation, 107
  preparation for showings, 75–79
Seller's market, 113–114
  buyer's agents in, 114–117
  client questions in, 115
  personal reference
  letter in, 115–117
Senses, appealing to, during
  showings, 85–89
Showings
  after death of homeowner, 100–101
  appeals to senses during, 85–89
  sight, 85–86
  smell, 86
  sound, 87
  taste, 87
  touch, 87–88
  children and, 75
  clutter and, 76–79
  daytime, 85
  during holiday seasons, 86
  nighttime, 85
  pets and, 75
  preparation for, 70, 75–79, 81–89
  radio and, 76
  refreshments at, 87
  scheduling of, 88
  television and, 76
  things to avoid, 75–77
  transportation to, 33
Sight, appeals to, during
  showings, 85–86
Slump, in market, 40–42, 114,
  117–118
Smell, appeals to, during
  showings, 86
Smiling, 34–35
Social skills, 123–124
Sound, appeals to, during

showings, 87–88
Spending limits, 36–37
Staging, 81–89, 101
Standardized tests, and school
  quality, 67
Success, Four E's of, 39–48
  Effort, 40–42, 47
  Enthusiasm, 46–47, 48
  Ethics, 43–46, 48
  Expertise, 42–43, 47–48, 49–62

T
Taste, appeals to, during
  showings, 87
Teamwork, 129–144
  in difficult times, 137–139
  and goals, 136–137
  strengths of players in, 133–136
Technology, 53–57, 125–126
Telemarketing, 30–31
Television, at showings, 76
Textures, appeals to, during
  showings, 87–88
Touch, appeals to, during
  showings, 87–88
Transportation, to showings, 33
Trust, earning, 96–97

W
World Wide Web, 53–54.
  See also Technology

About The Author

Myra Nourmand is the First Lady of Beverly Hills Real Estate. She is a top-producing broker for Nourmand and Associates, a real estate firm specializing in Los Angeles premiere properties.

Myra's life experiences have inspired her throughout her career. While raising her children, she became a licensed broker and nearly 20 years later, she continues to love her work everyday. A native of New York, the author earned her B.A. at SUNY-Buffalo. Myra and her husband, Saeed, have called Beverly Hills home for the last 30 years.

Learn More About Myra's Method

Visit Myra online at **myranourmand.com**. Once you're there you can order copies of her book, read her blog, see clips of her TV appearances, and view luxury properties throughout Los Angeles.